100 IRISH BALLADS VOL. 2

C[illegible]

The Publisher wishes to thank the National Library, Dublin, for their kind permission for use of the Photographs, Drawings and Engravings.

100 IRISH BALLADS VOLUME 2
ISBN 1 85720 011 X

BELIEVE ME, IF ALL THOSE ENDEARING YOUNG CHARMS

This song was written by Thomas Moore (1779–1852). It was dedicated to his wife who on contracting a skin disease feared Moore would no longer love her.

It is not while beauty and youth are thine own
And thy cheeks unprofaned by a tear
That the fervour and faith of a soul can be known
To which time will but make thee more dear.
No, the heart that has truly loved never forgets
But as truly loves on to the close
As the sun-flower turns on her God when he sets
The same look which she turned when he rose.

This song was collected by Patrick Joyce around 1840. Joyce thought the song originated from Donegal. Like Mrs. McGrath and The Kerry Recruit it was written as an anti-recruiting song.

ARTHUR McBRIDE

He said 'my young fellows if you will enlist
A guinea you quickly will have in your fist
And besides a crown for to kick up the dust
And drink the king's health in the morning'.
Had we been such fools as to take the advance
With the wee bit of money we'd have to run chance
'Do ye think it no scruples for to send us to France
Where we would be killed in the morning'.

He says 'My young fellows if I hear but one word
I instantly now will out with my sword
And into your bodies as strength will support
So now my gay devils take warning.'
But Arthur and I we took the odds
And we gave them no chance for to launch out their swords
Our whacking shillelaghs came over their heads
And paid them right smart in the morning.

As for the young drummer, we rifled his pouch
And we made a football of his rowdy-dou-dou
And into the ocean to rock and to roll
And barring the day it's returning.
As for the rapier that hung by his side
We flung it as far as we could in the tide
To the devil I pit you, says Arthur McBride
To temper your steel in the morning.

THE KERRY RECRUIT

This is an anti-recruiting song. It is similar to "The Recruiting Sergeant" written by Seamus O'Farrell in 1915. Anyone heard singing this or any other anti-recruiting songs was liable to six months' imprisonment.

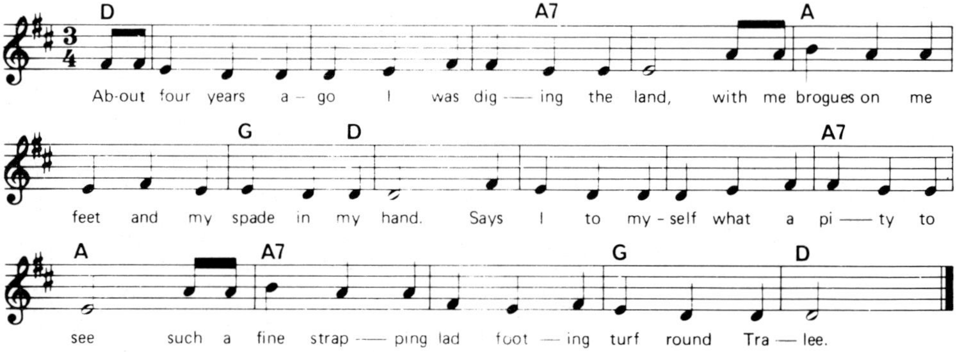

So I buttoned my brogues and shook hands with my spade
And I went to the fair like a dashing young blade
When up comes a sergeant and asks me to 'list
'Arra Sergeant, a gra, put the bob in my fist.

And the first thing they gave me it was a red coat
With a wide strap of leather to tie round my throat
They gave me a square thing, I asked what was that
And they told me it was a cockade for my hat.

The next thing they gave me, they called it a gun
With powder and shot and a place for my thumb
And first she spit fire and then she spit smoke
Lord, she gave a great lep and my shoulder near broke.

The next place they sent me was down to the sea
On board of a war-ship bound for the Crimea
Three sticks in the middle all rowled round with sheets
Faith, she walked thro' the water without any feet.

We fought at the Alma, likewise Inkermann
But the Russians they whaled us at the Redan
In scaling the walls there myself lost my eye
And a big Russian bullet ran off with my thigh.

It was there I lay bleeding, stretched on the cold ground
Heads, legs and arms were scattered all around
Says I, if my man or my cleaveens were nigh
They'd bury me decent and raise a loud cry.

They brought me the doctor, who soon staunched my blood
And he gave me an elegant leg made of wood
They gave me a medal and tenpence a day
Contented with Sheela, I'll live on half-pay.

A REAL KERRY MAN

FIDDLERS GREEN

This is a sailor's song written by W. Connolly.

Now Fiddler's Green is a place I heard tell
Where the fishermen go if they don't go to hell
Where the skies are all clear and the dolphins do play
And the cold coast of Greenland is far, far away.

When you get on the docks and the long trip is through
There's pubs and there's clubs and there's lassies there too
Where the girls are all pretty and the beer it is free
And there's bottles of rum growing from every tree.

Now, I don't want a harp nor a halo, not me
Just give me a breeze and a good rolling sea
I'll play me old squeeze-box as we sail along
With the wind in the riggin to sing me a song.

Published by HEDLEY MUSIC GROUP LTD

PADDY LAY BACK

Oh, Paddy lay Back – (Paddy lay Back) take in the stack (take in the stack)
Take a turn around the capstan, heave up all (heave up all)
About ship stations boys be handy (be handy)
For we're bound for Valiporizor round the Horn (round the Horn).

Now some of our fellows had been drinking (been drinking)
And me meself was heavy on the booze (on the booze)
So I sat upon me old sea chest a thinking (a thinking)
I'll just turn in and have meself a snooze (have a snooze).

Well I wished I was in the Jolly Sailors (Sailors)
Along with Irish Paddies drinking beer (drinking beer)
Then I thought what a jolly lot are sailors (sailors)
And with me flipper I wiped away a tear (wiped a tear).

Cont......

Chorus: –

Well we got all the tugs up along side (along side)
They towed us from the warf and out to sea (out to sea)
With half the crew just hanging o'er the ships side (the ships side)
And the bloody row that started sickened me (sickened me).

Well the bowsen he said he couldn't savey us (savey us)
The crews were speaking lingos all galore (all galore)
So the only thing the old man could do was (could do was)
Pay us ugly sailors off and ship some more (ship some more).

DEAR OLD IRELAND

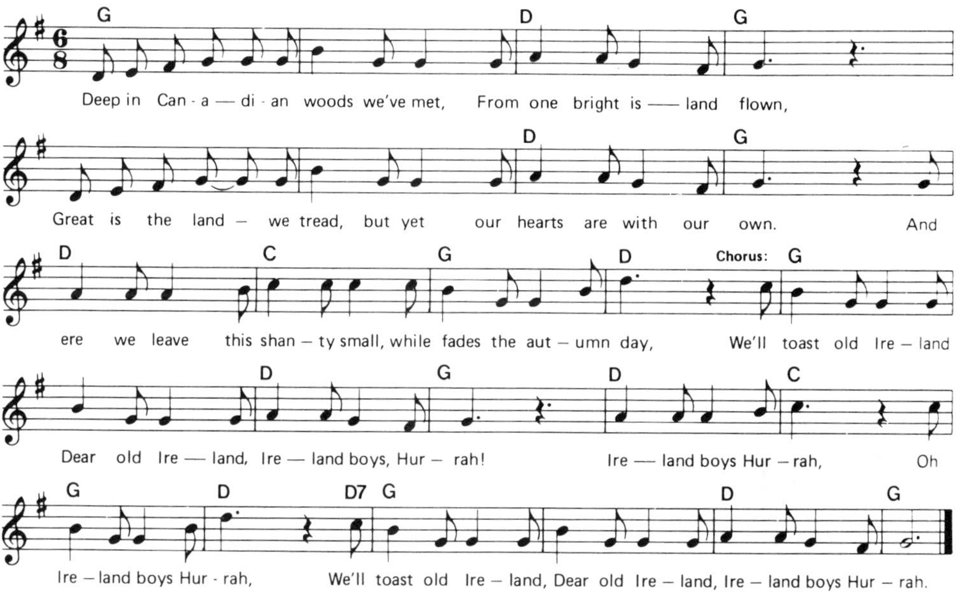

We've heard her faults a hundred times, The new ones and the old.
In songs and sermons, rants and rhymes, Enlarged some fifty-fold.
But take them all, the great and small, And this we've got to say:—
Here's dear old Ireland! good old Ireland! Ireland, boys, Hurrah!

We know that brave and good men tried, to snap her rusty chain.
The patriots suffered, martyrs died, And all, 'tis said, in vain:
But no boy, no! a glance will show, How far they've won their way—
Here's good old Ireland! loved old Ireland! Ireland, boys, Hurrah!

We've seen the wedding and the wake, The patron and the fair;
And lithe young frames at the dear old games, In the kindly Irish air.
And the loud "Hurroo", we have heard it too, And a thundering "Clear the way!"
Here's gay old Ireland! dear old Ireland! Ireland, boys, Hurrah!

And well we know in cool grey eyes, When the hard day's work is o'er,
How soft and sweet are the words that greet, The friends who meet once more.
With "Mary Machree!" and "My Pat, 'tis he!" And "My own heart night and day!"
Ah, fond old Ireland! dear old Ireland! Ireland, boys, Hurrah!

And happy and bright are the groups that pass, from their peaceful homes, for miles
O'er fields and roads, and hills, to Mass, When Sunday morning smiles!
And deep the zeal their true hearts feel, when low they kneel and pray,
O, dear old Ireland! blest old Ireland! Ireland, boys, Hurrah!

But deep in Canadian woods, we've met, And we never may see again
The dear old isle where our hearts are set, And our first fond hopes remain!
But come, fill up another cup, And with every sup let's say:
"Here's loved old Ireland! good old Ireland! Ireland, boys, Hurrah!"

THE GALWAY RACES

This song is a celebration of the annual horse racing event which takes place in Galway on the West coast of Ireland.

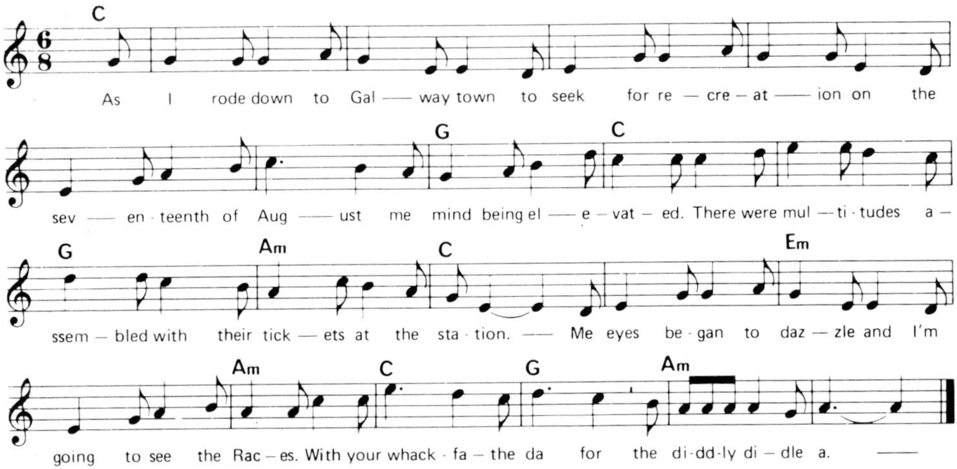

There were passengers from Limerick and more from Tipperary
Boys from Connemara and a flair of married ladies
People from Cork City who were loyal, true and faithful
Who brought home the Fenian prisoners from dying in foreign nations
With your whack-fa-the-da, for the diddly-diddle-day.

It's there you'll see the pipers and the fiddlers competing
The nimble-footed dancers a-tripping over the daisies
There were others crying cigars and likes, and bills for all the races
With the colours of the jockeys and the price and horses' ages
With your whack-fa-the-da, for the diddly-diddle-day.

It's there you'll see the jockeys and they're mounted out so stately
The pink, the blue, the orange and the green, the emblem of our Nation
When the bell was rung for starting, all the horses seemed impatient
I thought they never stood on ground their speed was so amazing
With your whack-fa-the-da, for the diddly-diddle-day.

There was half a million people there from all denominations
The Catholic, the Protestant, the Jew and Presbyterian
There was yet no animosity, no matter what persuasion
But sportsman hospitality and induce fresh acquaintance
With your whack-fa-the-da, for the diddly-diddle-day.

Written by Patrick J. McCall (1861–1919). This is a vicious and bloody song celebrating the defeat by Fiach McHugh O'Byrne of Lord Deputy Grey at Glenmalure in 1580.

FOLLOW ME UP TO CARLOW

See the swords of Glen Imaal, a flashing o'er the English pale
See all the children of the Gael beneath O'Byrne's banner
Rooster of a fighting stock would yet let a saxon cock
Crow out upon an Irish rock, fly up and teach him manners.

Repeat Chorus:–

Now from Tassagart to Clonmore, there flows a stream of Saxon gore
And great is Rory Óg O'More at sending loons to hades
White is sick and Grey has fled, now for Black Fitzwilliam's head
We'll send it over dripping red, to Liza and her ladies.

AN IRISH SOLDIER LADDIE

This song was written by Pat McGuigan who also wrote among other ballads "The Men Behind The Wire".

Said I to that soldier lad, would you take me to your Captain
It would be my pride and joy for to march with you today
My young brother fell at Cork and my son at Enniscorthy
To the noble Captain I did say

Repeat Chorus:–

As we marched back again in the shadow of the evening
With our banners flying low to the memory of the dead
Oh we came back to our homes but without our soldier laddie
But I still can hear those brave words he said.

Repeat Chorus:–

Published by WALTONS

This song was written by Dominic Behan, brother of Brendan. It tells the story of Fergus O'Hanlon from Ballybay, Co. Monaghan. He was killed during the Brookborough attack at the age of 17.

THE PATRIOT GAME

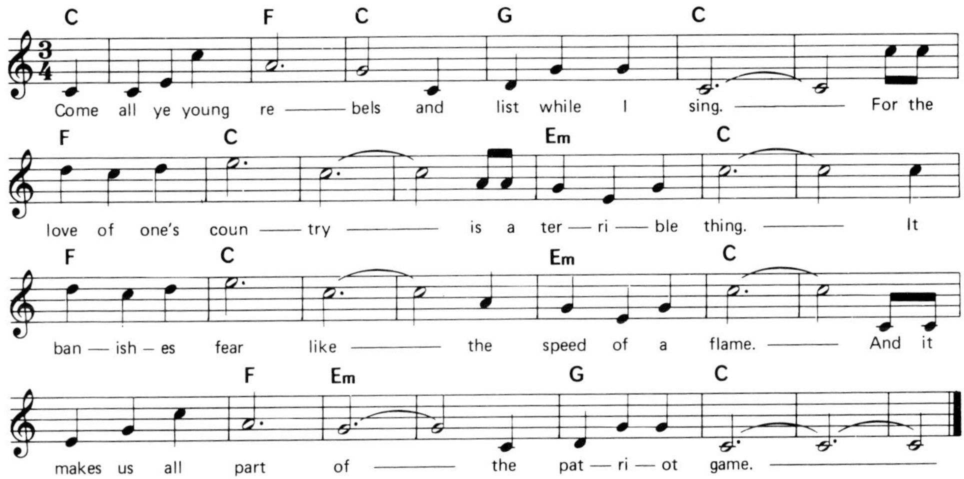

My name is O'Hanlon and I've just turned sixteen
My home is in Monaghan where I was weaned
I've learned all my life cruel England's to blame
So now I am part of the Patriot Game.

It's nearly two years since I wandered away
With the local battalion of the bold I.R.A.
For I read of our heroes and wanted the same
To play my part in the Patriot Game.

Now as I lie here, my body all holes
I think of those traitors who bargained and sold
I wish that my rifle had given the same
To those quislings who sold out the Patriot Game.

DUBLIN CASTLE

WHEN IRISH EYES ARE SMILING

Words by CHAUNCEY OLCOTT & GEO GRAFF JNR
Music by ERNEST BALL

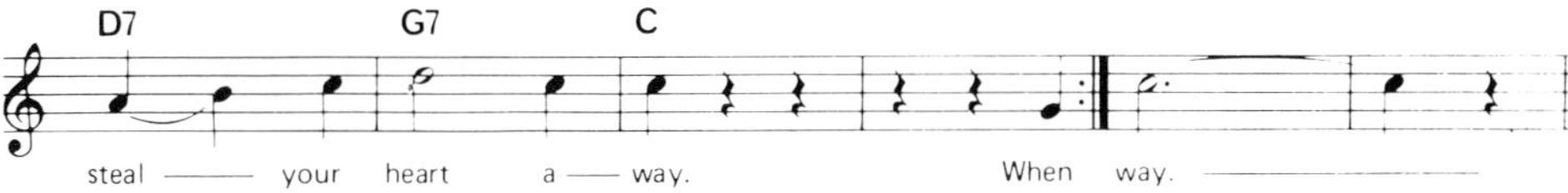

For your smile is a part, of the love in your heart,
And it makes even sunshine more bright
Like the linnet's sweet song, crooning all the day long,
Comes your laughter so tender and light.
For the spring-time of life is the sweetest of all,
There is ne'er a real care or regret;
And while spring-time is ours, throughout all of youth's hours,
Let us smile each chance we get.

Chrous:–

THE THREE FLOWERS

This is a modern song written by Norman G. Reddin. It concerns a famous guerilla fighter, Michael Dwyer, who lived in a cottage in the Glen of Imaal, in the Wicklow Mountains.

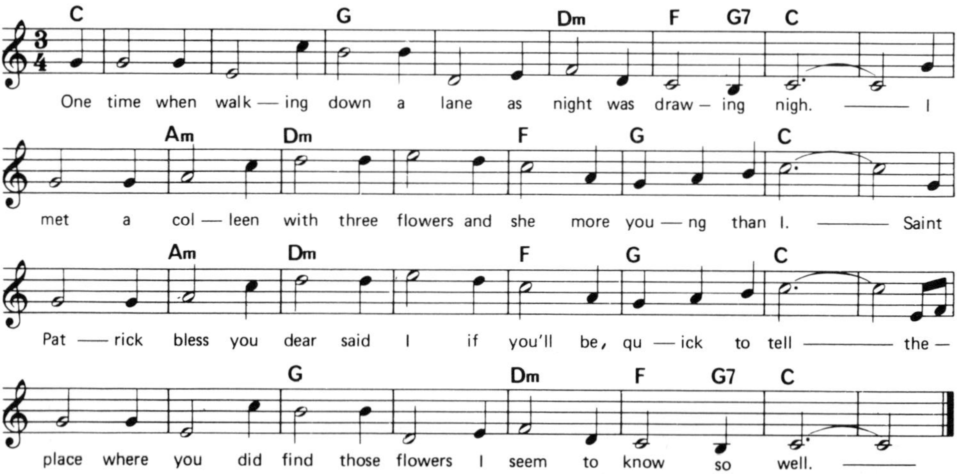

She took a flower and kissed it once, and softly said to me
This flower I found in Thomas Street, in Dublin fair said she
It's name is Robert Emmet, it's the youngest flower of all
And I keep it fresh beside my breast, though all the world should fall.

She took a flower and kissed it twice, and softly said to me
This flower comes from the Antrim Hills, outside Belfast said she
The name I call it is Wolfe Tone, the greatest flower of all
And I'll keep it fresh beside my breast, though all the world should fall.

She took a flower and kissed it thrice, and softly said to me
This flower comes from the Wicklow Hills, it's name is Dwyer said she
And Emmet, Tone and Dwyer, for I do love them all
And I keep them fresh beside my breast, though all the world should fall.

Published by WALTONS

EILEEN O'GRADY

Cont....

Now Eileen said, "No sir, with you I won't go, sir,
Don't think it ungrateful of me:
I'd rather go walking than have people talking,
You know what the story would be."
No Eileen, my jewel, don't treat me so cruel,
To treat me this way is a shame,
Give over your blarney and say I'm your Barney,
And don't keep me waiting in vain.

Chorus:–

AN IRISH JAUNTING CAR

THE BANKS OF MY OWN LOVELY LEE

And then in the springtime of laughter and song,
Can I ever forget the sweet hours
With the friends of my youth as we rambled along
'Mongst the green mossy banks and wild flowers.
Then too, when the evening sun's sinking to rest
Sheds its golden light over the sea
The maid with her lover the wild daisies pressed
On the banks of my own lovely Lee,
The maid with her lover the wild daisies pressed
On the banks of my own lovely Lee.

Cont.........

'Tis a beautiful land this dear isle of song
Its gems shed their light to the world.
And her faithful sons bore thro' ages of wrong,
The standard St. Patrick unfurled.
Oh! would I were there with the friends I love best
And my fond bosom's partner with me
We'd roam thy banks over, and when weary we'd rest
By thy waters, my own lovely Lee,
We'd roam thy banks over, and when weary we'd rest
By thy waters, my own lovely Lee.

Oh what joys should be mine ere this life should decline
To seek shells on thy sea-gilded shore.
While the steel-feathered eagle, oft splashing the brine
Brings longing for freedom once more.
Oh all that on earth I wish for or crave
Is that my last crimson drop be for thee,
To moisten the grass of my forefathers' grave
On the banks of my own lovely Lee,
To moisten the grass of my forefathers' grave
On the banks of my own lovely Lee.

Published by SHANAHANS

THE MARDYKE, CORK.

LOUGH SHEELIN SIDE

It was at the dance in the village green
I met young Eileen my own cailin
I took young Eileen my fond young bride
To my cottage home by Lough Sheelin side.

But our good dreams were too good to last
The landlord came our home to blast
And he no mercy on us did show
As he turned us out in the blinding snow.

Will no one open to us a door
In case that vengeance on them might fall
'Twas there she fainted 'twas there she died
As the snow fell fast by Lough Sheelin side.

They dug her grave in the churchyard low
It was in the spring time when the daisies grow
Sad tears were shed for my fond young bride
Who's sleeping now by Lough Sheelin side.

Farewell old Ireland and Eileen too
My ship is ready I bid adieu
For I must leave for the ocean wide
From my true love's grave by Lough Sheelin side.

Published by WALTONS

THE MEETING OF THE WATERS

Written by Thomas Moore (1779–1852). Moore was born in Aungier St. Dublin, the son of a Grocer. "The Meeting of the Waters" is the meeting of the Avonmor and Avonbeg in Avoca, Co. Wicklow.

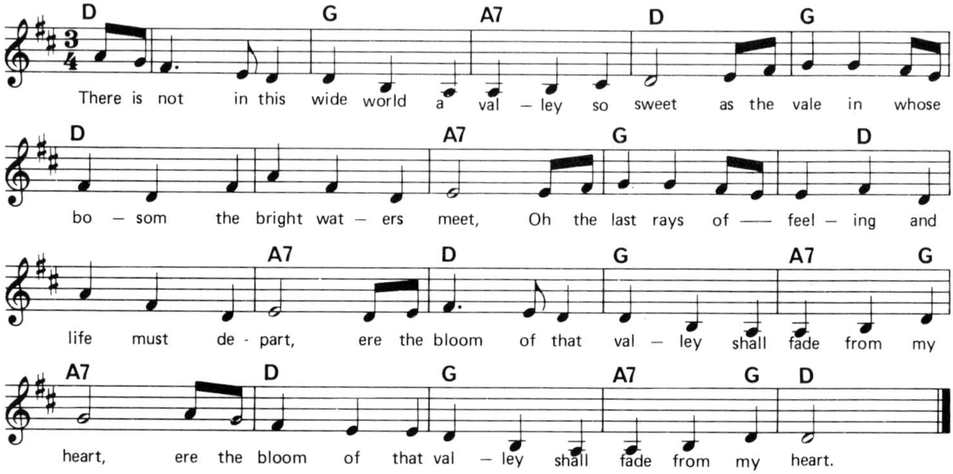

Yet it was not that nature had shed o'er the scene
Her purest of crystal and brightest of green
'Twas not her soft magic of streamlet or hill
Oh! no – it was something more exquisite still.

'Twas that friends, the beloved of my bosom, were near
Who made every dear scene of enchantment more dear
And who felt how the best charms of Nature improve
When we see them reflected from looks that we love.

Sweet Vale of Avoca! how calm could I rest
In thy bosom of shade, with the friends I love best
Where the storms that we feel in this cold world should cease
And our hearts, like thy waters, be mingled in peace.

MEETING OF THE WATERS, AVOCA, CO. WICKLOW
Immortalised by Thomas Moore in his famous song

This song was written in 1973 by Michael McConnell. It is a slow sad song lamenting the fact that Ireland is still not a free country.

ONLY OUR RIVERS

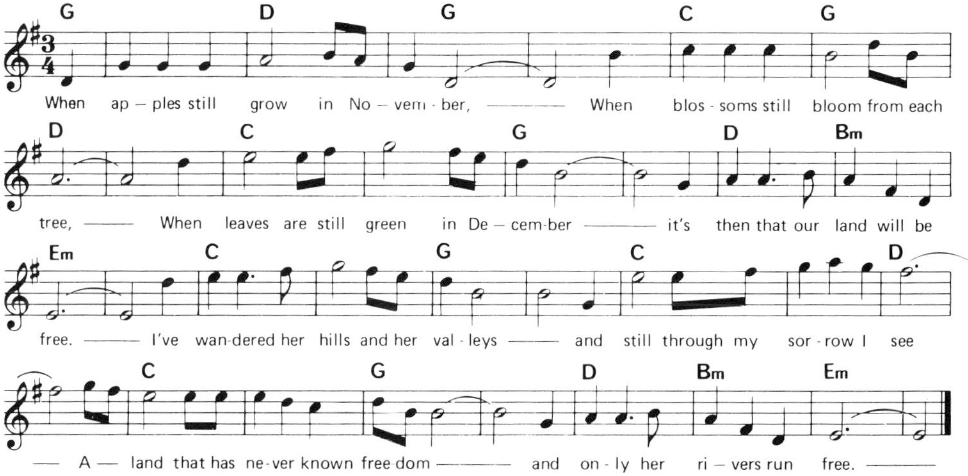

I drink to the death of her manhood
Those men who'd rather have died
Than to live in cold chains of bondage
To bring back their rights were denied
Oh where are you now when we need you
What burns where the flame used to be
Are ye gone like the snows of last winter
And will only our rivers run free?

How sweet is life, but we're crying
How mellow the wine that we're dry
How fragrant the rose, but it's dying
How gentle the wind, but it sighs
What good is in youth when it's ageing
What joy is in eyes that can't see
When there's sorrow in sunshine and flowers
And still only our rivers run free.

Words & Music by MICHAEL MacCONNELL

THE BARD OF ARMAGH

This song was probably written in the mid 19th century. The air is slow and sad and was also used in America for the "Streets of Laredo"

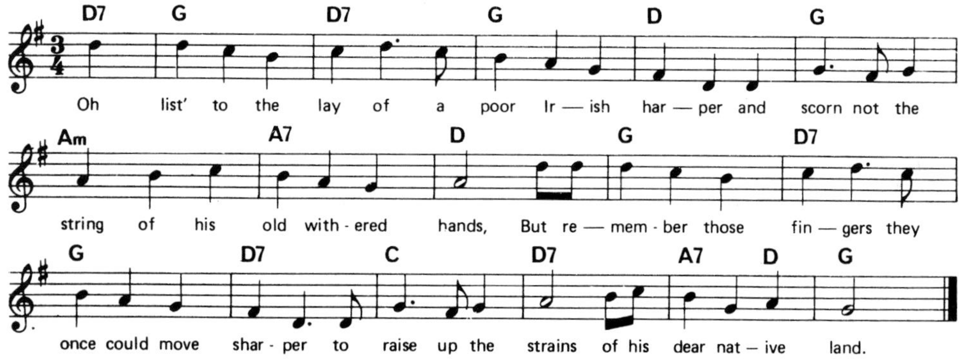

It was long before the shamrock, dear Isle's lovely emblem
Was crushed in its beauty by the Saxon's lion paw
And all the pretty colleens around me would gather
Call me their bold Phelim Brady, the Bard of Armagh.

How I love to muse on the days of my boyhood
Though four score and three years have fled by them
It's king's sweet reflection that every young joy
For the merry-hearted boys make the best of old men.

At a fair or a wake I would twist my shillelah
And trip through a dance with my brogues tied with straw
There, all the pretty maidens around me gather
Call me their bold Phelim Brady, the Bard of Armagh.

In truth I have wandered this wide world over
Yet Ireland's my home and a dwelling for me
And, oh, let the turf that my old bones shall cover
Be cut from the land that is trod by the free.

And when sergeant death in his cold arms doth embrace
And lull me to sleep with old Erin-go-bragh
By the side of my Kathleen, my dear pride, oh, place me
Then forget Phelim Brady, the Bard of Armagh.

I ONCE LOVED A LASS

When I saw my love go through the church door,
With bride and bride maidens, they made a fine show;
And I follow the man with my heart full of woe,
For now she is wed to another.

When I saw my love a-sit down to dine,
I sat down beside her and I poured out the wine;
And I drank to the lass that should have been mine,
But now she is wed to another.

The men of yon forest, they ask it of me,
How many strawberries grow in the salt sea?
And I ask of them back with a tear in my eye,
How many ships sail in the forest?

So dig me a grave and dig it so deep
And cover it over with flowers so sweet;
And I'll turn in for to take a long sleep,
And maybe in time I'll forget her.

So they dug him a grave and they dug it so deep;
They covered it over with flowers so sweet.
And he's turned in for to take a long sleep,
And maybe by now he's forgotten.

LOVERS

And as lovers lie sleeping, I find myself travelling towards you.
The morning arises, the wind is as soft as a sigh.
And whatever's before me, is nothing to what I have come through,
The pain and the passion, the tears and the laughs and the lies.

My darling once told me, that loving was better than living;
But I told her survival for me, was the easier game.
I couldn't live with her, now it's I can't live without her;
I thought I'd feel different, but somehow I still feel the same.

Romeo tells me that Juliet can't live without him,
And Ophelia's crazy for Hamlet who wants to be king.
And away in the distance, Mark Anthony loves Cleopatra,
As Portia sits silent, soliloquizing in the wings.

So if lovers are losers, what price the game we are playing?
And what price the man, who has not got the money to pay?
And the silence of angels means praying is just an illusion
For the lost and the lonely, and those who have nothing to say.

Repeat first verse:–

The 4th verse of this song has been omited from the cassette.

Words & Music by ADRIAN MANNERING
Published by BOLD TIMES MUSIC

NOVA SCOTIA

I grieve to leave my native land
I grieve to leave my comrades all
And my parents whom I held so dear
And the bonny bonny lassie that I do adore.

Chorus:–

The drums do beat and the wars do alarm
And the captain's call we must obey,
So farewell, farewell to Nova Scotia's charms
For it's early in the morning I'll be far far away.

Chorus:–

I have three Brothers and they are at rest
And their arms are folded on their breast,
But a poor simple sailor just like me
Must be tossed and driven on the dark blue sea.

Chorus:–

MARY MAC

Well this little lass she has a lot of class
Got a lot of brass and her father thinks I'm gas
And I'd be a silly ass for to let the matter pass
My father says she suits me really fairly.

Chorus:–

Mary and her mother go an awful lot together
In fact you'd hardly ever see the one without the other
And the people wonder whether it is Mary or her Mother
Or the both of them together that I'm courting.

Chorus:–

The Wedding's on a Wednesday and everything's arranged
Soon her name will change to mine unless her mind is changed
And with making the arrangements I'm just about deranged
Marriage is an awful undertaking.

Chorus:–

Sure to be a grand affair and grander than a fair
There's going to be a coach and pair for every pair that's there
We'll dine upon the finest fair I'm sure to get me share
If I don't I'll be very much mistaken.

SEAN SOUTH

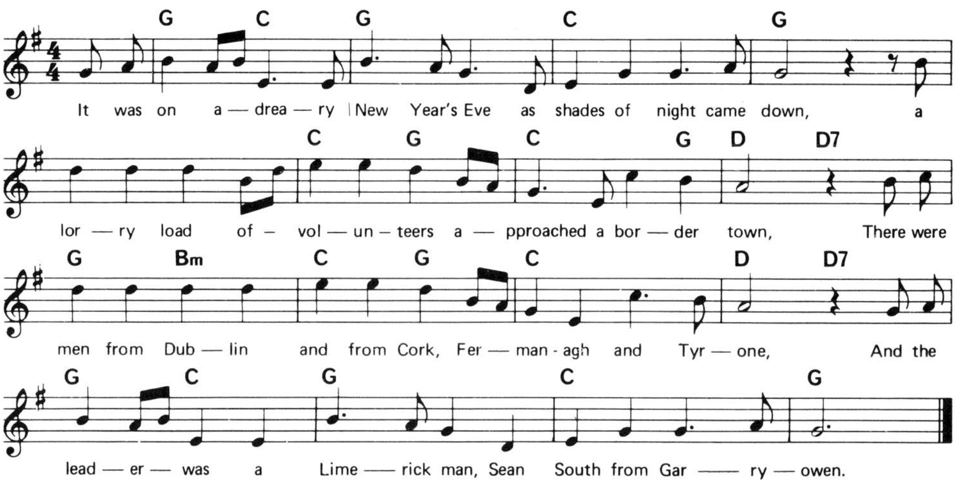

And as they moved along the street up to the barracks door
They scorned the dangers they would meet, the fate that lay in store.
They were fighting for old Ireland's cause to claim their very own,
And the leader was a Limerick man, Sean South from Garryowen.

But the sergeant spied their daring plan, he spied them through the door.
With their sten guns and their rifle (butts), a hail of death did roar.
And when that awful night was past, two men lay cold as stone,
There was one from near the border and one from Garryowen.

No more they'll hear the seagulls cry o'er the murmuring Shannon tide,
For they fell beneath a northern sky, brave Hanlon by their side.
They have gone to join that gallant band of Plunkett, Pearce and Tone,
Another martyr for old Ireland, Sean South from Garryowen.

THE BROAD BLACK BRIMMER

It was the uniform been worn by me father long ago
When he reached me mothers homestead on the run
It was the uniform me father wore in that little church below
When oul Father Mac. he blessed the pair as one
And after truce and treaty and the parting of the ways
He wore it when he marched out with the rest
And when they bore his body down that rugged heather braes
They placed the broad black brimmer on his breast.

Chorus:–

Published by OUTLET RECORDING CO. LTD.

TIPPING IT UP TO NANCY

She went down to the chemist shop some remedies for to buy,
'Have you anything in your chemist shop to make me old man blind?

Chorus:–

'Give him eggs and marrowbones and make him suck them all,
Before he has the last one sucked, he won't see you at all.'

Chorus:–

She gave him eggs and marrowbones and made him suck them all,
Before he had the last one sucked, he couldn't see her at all.

Chorus:–

'If in this world I cannot see, here I cannot stay.
I'd rather go and drown myself,' 'Come on,' says she, 'and I'll show you the way'.

Chorus:–

She led him to the river, she led him to the brim,
But sly enough of Martin, it was him that shoved her in.

Chorus:–

She swam through the river, she swam through the brine,
'Oh Martin, dear Martin don't leave me behind',
'Yerra shut up outa that ye silly aul fool', ye know poor Martin is blind'.

Chorus:–

There's nine in me family and none of them is my own,
I wish that each and every man would come and claim his own.

Chorus:–

RAGLAN ROAD

On Grafton Street in November we tripped lightly along the ledge
Of a deep ravine where can be seen the worth of passion play.
The Queen of Hearts still making tarts, and I not making hay,
Oh, I loved too much and by such and such, is happiness thrown away.

I gave her gifts of the mind, I gave her the secret signs
That's known to the artists who have known the true gods of sound and stone
And her words and tint without stint, I gave her poems to say,
With her own name there and her own dark hair, like clouds over fields of May.

On a quiet street where old ghosts meet, I see her walking now
Away from me so hurriedly, my reason must allow.
That I had loved not as I should, a creature made of clay,
When the angel woos the clay he'll lose, his wings at the dawn of day.

Words & Music by PATRICK KAVANAGH

THE BONNY BOY

This is a song of Scottish origin. It tells the story of a girl of 21 who is married at the instigation of her father to a boy of 16 who dies after the first year of their marriage.

Oh father, dear father, I think you did me wrong
For to go and get me married to one who is so young
For he is but sixteen and I am twenty-one
But the bonny boy is young but he's growing.

Oh daughter, dear daughter, I did not do you wrong
For to go and get you married to one who is so young
He will be a match for you when I am dead and gone
Oh the bonny boy is young but he's growing.

Oh father, dear father, I'll tell you what I'll do
I'll send my love to college for another year or two
And all around his college cap I'll bind a ribbon blue
To show the other girls that he's married.

'Twas at the age of sixteen years he was a married man
And at the age of seventeen, the father of a son
But at the age of eighteen, o'er his grave the grass grew high
Cruel death put an end to his growing.

I will buy my love a shroud of the finest Holland brown
And whilst I am a weaving it the tears they will flow down
For once I had a true-love, but now he's lying low
And I'll nurse his bonny boy while he's growing.

An exile song associated with Slieve Gallion Brae on the Sperrin Mountains in Counties Derry and Tyrone.

SLIABH GALLION BRAE

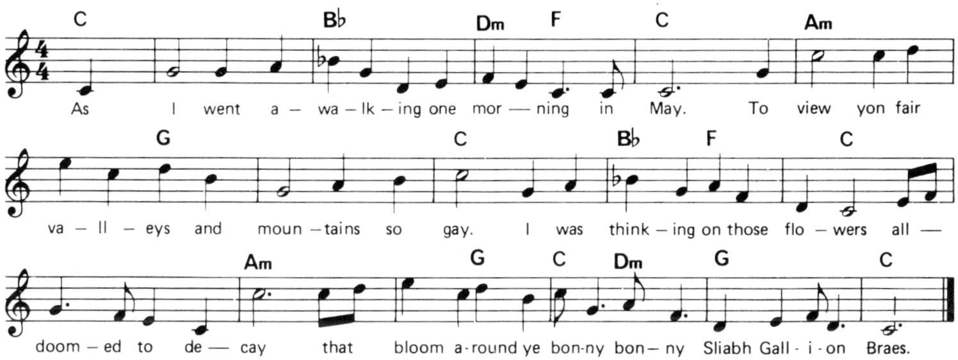

How oft in the morning with my dog and my gun
I roam through the glens for joy and for fun
But those days are now all over and I must go away
So farewell unto ye, bonny, bonny, Sliabh Gallion Braes.

How oft of an evening and the sun in the West
I roved hand in hand with the one I loved best
But the hopes of youth are vanished and now I'm far away
So farewell unto ye, bonny, bonny, Sliabh Gallion Braes.

Oh! it was not the want of employment at home
That caused us poor exiles in sorrow to roam
But those tyrannising landlords, they would not let us stay
So farewell unto ye, bonny, bonny, Sliabh Gallion Braes.

THREE SCORE AND TEN

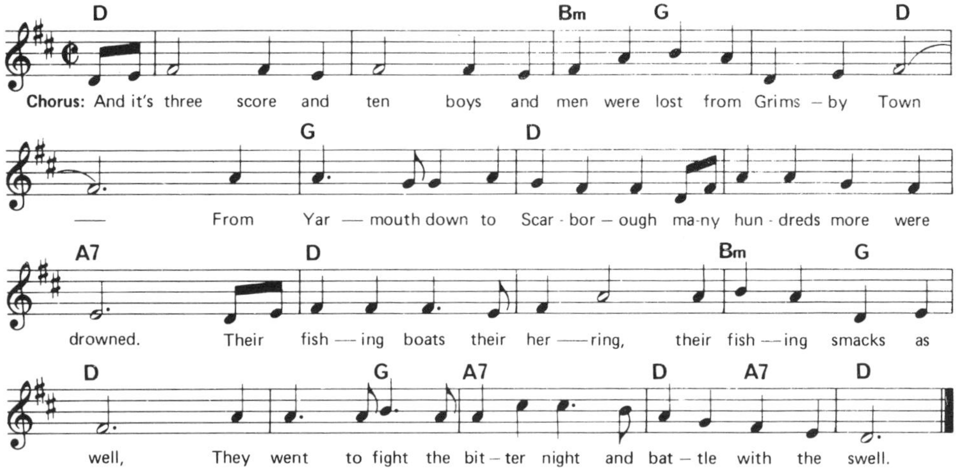

Me thinks I see s host of craft spreading their sails a-lea
As down the Humber they did lye, bound for the cold North Sea
Me thinks I see's a wee small craft, and crew with hearts so brave
They want to earn their daily bread, upon the restless waves.

Repeat Chorus:–

October night brought such a sight, 'twas never seen before
There were masts and yards of broken spars washed-up on the shore
There was many a heart of sorrow, there was many a heart so brave
There was many a true and noble lad to find a watery grave.

THE JUICE OF THE BARLEY

Well when I was a gossoon of eight years old or so
With me turf and me primer to school I did go
To a dusty old school-house without any door
Where lay the school master blind drunk on the floor.

Repeat Chorus:–

At the learning I wasn't such a genius I'm thinking
But I soon bet the master entirely at drinking
Not a wake or a wedding for five miles around
But meself in the corner was sure to be found.

Repeat Chorus:–

One Sunday the priest thread me our from the altar
Saying, "you'll end up your days with your neck in a halter
And you'll dance a fine jig between heaven and hell",
And his words they did frighten me, the truth for to tell.

Repeat Chorus:–

So the very next morning as the dawn it did break
I went down to the vestry, the pledge for to take,
And there in that room sat the priests in a bunch
'Round a big roaring fire drinking tumblers of punch.

Repeat Chorus:–

Well from that day to this I have wandered alone
I'm jack of all trades and a master of none
With the sky for me roof and the earth for me floor
And I'll dance out me days drinking whiskey galore.

Repeat Chorus:–

MUSH MUSH

Oh 'twas there I learned all my courtin', Many lessons I took in the art;
Till Cupid, the blackguard, while sportin', An arrow drove straight thro' my heart.
Molly O'Connor, she lived just forninst me, And tender lines to her I wrote,
If you dare say one hard word agin her, I'll tread on the tail of your coat.
Chorus:—
But a blackguard called Mickey Maloney, Came and stole her affections away,
For he'd money and I hadn't any, So I sent him a challenge next day.
In the evening we met at the woodbine, The Shannon we crossed in a boat,
And I lathered him with my shillelah, For he trod on the tail of my coat.
Chorus:—
Oh, my fame went abroad thro' the nation, And folks came a flocking to see,
And they cried out without hesitation, "You're a fightin' man, Billy McGee."
I have claned out the Finegan faction, And I've licked all the Murphys afloat,
If you're in for a row or a ruction, Just tread on the tail of my coat.
Chorus:—

ROSIN THE BOW

When I'm dead and laid out on the counter; A voice you will hear from below
Saying, 'send down a hogshead of whiskey; To drink with old Rosin the Bow'.
Chorus:–
To drink with old Rosin the Bow, me lad; To drink with old Rosin the Bow
Saying, 'send down a hogshead of whiskey; To drink with old Rosin the Bow.

And get a half dozen stout fellows; And stack them all up in a row
Let them drink out of half gallon bottles; To the memory of Rosin the Bow.
Chorus:–
To the memory of Rosin the Bow, me lad; To the memory of Rosin the Bow
Let them drink out of half gallon bottles; To the memory of Rosin the Bow.

Get this half dozen stout fellows; And let them all stagger and go
And dig a great hole in the meadow; And in it put Rosin the Bow.
Chorus:–
And in it put Rosin the Bow, me lad; And in it put Rosin the Bow
And dig a great hole in the meadow; And in it put Rosin the Bow.

Get ye a couple of bottles; Put one at me head and me toe
With a diamond ring scratch upon them; The name of old Rosin the Bow.
Chorus:–
The name of old Rosin the Bow, me lad; The name of old Rosin the Bow
With a diamond ring scratch upon them; The name of old Rosin the Bow.

I feel that old tyrant approaching; That cruel remorseless old foe
And I lift up me glass in his honour; Take a drink with old Rosin the Bow.
Chorus:–
Take a drink with old Rosin the Bow, me lad; Take a drink with old Rosin the Bow
And I lift up me glass in his honour; Take a drink with old Rosin the Bow.

THE VALLEY OF KNOCKANURE

This Ballad tells the story of Jeremiah Lyons, Patrick Dalton and Patrick Walsh who were surrounded and killed by the Black and Tans at Gortagleann, Co. Kerry. It was written by a native of Kerry, Brian McMahon.

There was Lyons and Walsh and the Dalton boy; They were young and in their prime
They rambled to a lonely spot where the Black and Tans did hide
The Republic bold they did uphold, tho' outlawed on the moor
And side by side they fought and died in the Valley of Knockanure.

It was on a neighbouring hillside, we listened in hushed dismay
In every house, in every town a young girl knelt to pray
They're closing in around them now, with rifle fire so sure
And Lyons is dead and young Dalton's down, in the Valley of Knockanure.

But e'er the guns could seal his fate, young Walsh had spoken thro'
With a prayer to God, he spurned the sod, as against the hill he flew
The bullets tore his flesh in two, yet he cried with voice so sure
"Revenge I'll get for my comrade's death, in the Valley of Knockanure."

The summer sun is sinking low behind the field and lea
The pale moonlight is shining bright far off beyond Tralee
The dismal stars and the clouds afar are darkening o'er the moor
And the banshee cried when young Dalton died, in the Valley of Knockanure.

Published by WALTONS

SHE MOVED THRO' THE FAIR

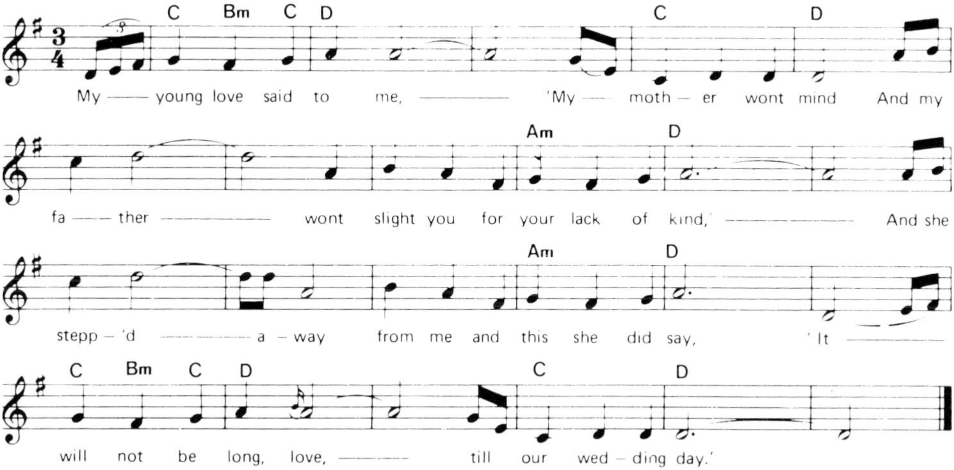

She went away from me, and moved through the fair,
And fondly I watched her, move here and move there,
Then she went homeward with one star awake –
As the swan in the evening moves over the lake.

The people were saying no two were e'er wed,
But one had a sorrow that never was said,
She went away from me with her goods and her gear,
And that was the last that I saw of my dear.

I dreamed it last night, my dear love came in,
So softly she came that her feet made no din,
She laid her hand on me, and this she did say:
'It will not be long, love, 'till our wedding day.'

THE HARP THAT ONCE THROUGH TARA'S HALLS

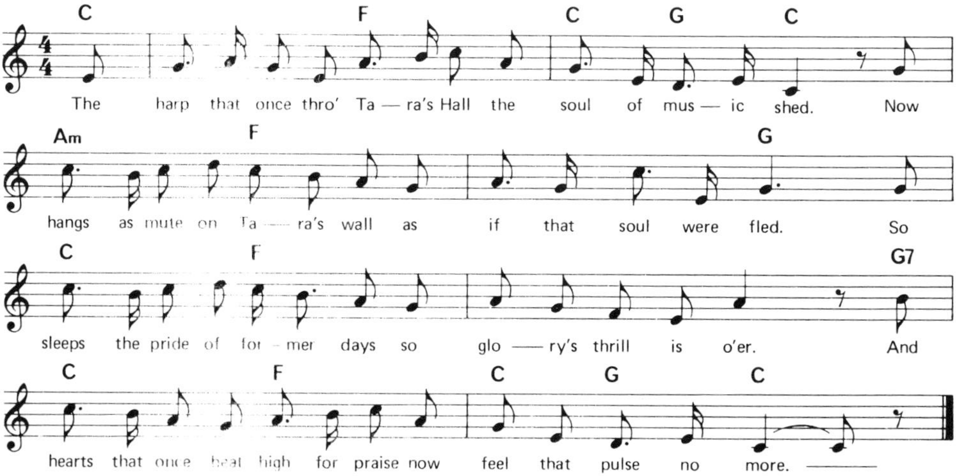

No more to chiefs and ladies bright, the harp of Tara swells
The chord alone, that breaks at night, it's tale of ruin tells
This freedom now so seldom wakes, the only throb she gives
Is when some heart indignant breaks, to show that still she lives.

CROPPIES STONE, TARA HILL

IRISH MOLLY O

Molly dear now did you hear I furnished up the flat
Three little cosy rooms with bath and 'welcome' on the mat.
It's five pounds down and two a week, we'll soon be out of debt,
It's all complete except they haven't brought the cradle yet.

Chorus:–

Molly dear and did you hear what all the neighbours say,
About the hundred sovereigns you have safely stowed away.
They say that's why I love you, Ah but Molly that's a shame.
If you had only ninety-nine, I'd love you just the same.

TRADITIONAL
Arranged by ALFRED MOFFAT and FRANK KIDSON

LET HIM GO, LET HIM TARRY

Chorus:–

Let him go let him tarry, let him sink or let him swim
He doesn't care for me nor I don't care for him.
He can go and get another and I hope he will enjoy
For I'm going to marry a far nicer boy.

He wrote me a letter saying he was very bad.
I sent him back an answer saying I was awful glad.
He wrote to me another saying he was well and strong,
But I care no more about him than the ground he walks upon.

Repeat Chorus:–

Some of his friends had a good kind wish for me,
Others of his friends they could hang me on a tree.
But soon I'll let them see my love, and soon I'll let them know
That I can get a new sweetheart on any grounds I go.

Repeat Chorus:–

He can go to his old mother now and set her mind at ease,
I hear she is an old, old woman, very hard to please.
It's slighting me and talking ill is what she's always done,
Because that I was courting her great big ugly son.

Repeat Chorus:–

THE MERMAID

Then up spoke the captain of our gallant ship; And a fine old man was he
"This fishy mermaid has warned me of our doom; We shall sink to the bottom of the sea."

Repeat Chorus:–

Then up spoke the mate of our gallant ship; And a fine spoken man was he
Saying "I have a wife in Brooklyn by the sea; And tonight a widow she will be."

Repeat Chorus:–

Then up spoke the cabin-boy of our gallant ship; And a brave young lad was he
"Oh I have a sweetheart in Salem by the sea; And tonight she'll be weeping for me."

Repeat Chorus:–

Then up spoke the cook of our gallant ship; And a crazy old butcher was he
"I care much more for my pots and my pans; Than I do for the bottom of the sea."

Repeat Chorus:–

Then three times 'round spun our gallant ship; And three times 'round spun she
Three times round spun our gallant ship; And she sank to the bottom of the sea.

Repeat Chorus:–

McALPINE'S FUSILIERS

This song was written by Dominic Behan, (brother of Brendan). It concerns Irishmen who emigrated to England to work on the building sites and motorways.

I stripped to the skin with darkie Finn; Way down upon the Isle of Grain
With horse-face O'Toole, we knew the rule; No money if you stopped for rain
McAlpine's God was a well-filled hod; Your shoulders cut to bits and seared
And woe to he who looked for tea, with McAlpine's Fusiliers.

I remember the day that the Bear O'Shea, fell into a concrete stairs
What horse-face said when he saw him dead; It wasn't what the rich call prayers
I'm a navvy short was the one retort, that reached unto my ears
When the going's rough, then you must be tough, with McAlpine's Fusiliers.

I've worked till the sweat nearly had me bet, with Russian, Czech and Pole
On shuddering jams up the hydro dams, or underneath the Thames in a hole
I grabbed it hard and I've got me cards, and many a ganger's fist across me ears
If you value your life, you won't join, by cripes, with McAlpine's Fusiliers.

Words & Music by D. BEHAN

ON THE ONE ROAD

Tinker, tailor – every mother's son
Butcher, baker – shouldering his gun.
Rich man, poor man – every man in line
All together, just like Auld Lang Syne!

Night is darkest just before the dawn.
From dissensions, Ireland is reborn.
Soon, will all United Irishmen,
See our land a Nation Once Again!

Published by WALTONS

THE OULD TRIANGLE

This song, written by Brendan Behan for his play "The Quare Fellow" is set in Mountjoy Prison. Dublin has two Canals – The Royal on the North side and The Grand on the South side.

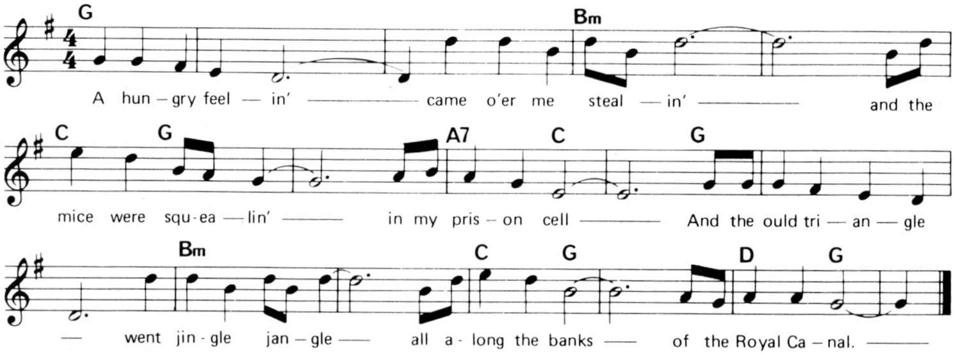

To begin the morning the warder bawling; 'Get out of bed and clean up your cell'
And that old triangle went jingle jangle, along the banks of the Royal Canal.

On a fine spring morning the lag lay dreaming, the seagulls wheeling high above the wall
And that old triangle went jingle jangle, along the banks of the Royal Canal.

The screw was peeping and the lag was sleeping, while he lay weeping for his girl Sal
And that old triangle went jingle jangle, along the banks of the Royal Canal.

The wind was rising and the day declining, as I lay pining in my prison cell
And that old triangle went jingle jangle, along the banks of the Royal Canal.

The day was dying and the wind was sighing, as I lay crying in my prison cell
And that old triangle went jingle jangle, along the banks of the Royal Canal.

In the female prison there are seventy women, I wish it was with them that I did dwell
And that old triangle could go jingle jangle, along the banks of the Royal Canal.

SACKVILLE ST. DUBLIN (now O'CONNELL ST.)
Nelson's Pillar (Admiral Nelson) was blown-up, 7th Mar. 1966

LIMERICK YOU'RE A LADY

Limerick you're a lady etc ....

The difference time has made, to travellers on their way,
Seeking out the beauty of our lands.
At shrines the children play, and bells ring out to say,
Thank God we're living just to feel the freedom of each day.

Limerick you're a lady etc ....

While waking in the arms of distant water,
A new day finds me far away from home.

Limerick you're a lady etc ....

Words & Music by DENNIS ALLEN
Published by EMMA MUSIC

MY SINGING BIRD

If I could lure my singing bird from its own cosy nest.
If I could catch my singing bird, I'd warm it on my breast,
And on my heart my singing bird would sing itself to rest,
Ah ——————— would sing itself to rest.

THE FIELDS OF ATHENRY

By a lonely prison wall
I heard a young man calling
Nothing matters Mary when you're free,
Against the Famine and the Crown
I rebelled they ran me down
Now you must raise our child with dignity.

Chorus:–

By a lonely harbour wall
She watched the last star falling
As that prison ship sailed out against the sky
Sure she'll wait and hope and pray
For her love in Botany Bay
It's so lonely round the fields of Athenry.

Chorus:–

Words & Music by PETE ST JOHN

Published by PETE ST JOHN/CELTIC SONGS

THE BOYS FROM THE COUNTY ARMAGH

I've travelled that part of the County, Through Newtown, Forkhill, Crossmaglen.
Around by the Gap of Mount Norris, And home by Blackwater again.
Where girls are so gay and so hearty, None fairer you'll find near or far,
But where are the boys that can court them, Like the boys from the County Armagh.

REPEAT CHORUS:–

Published by WALTONS

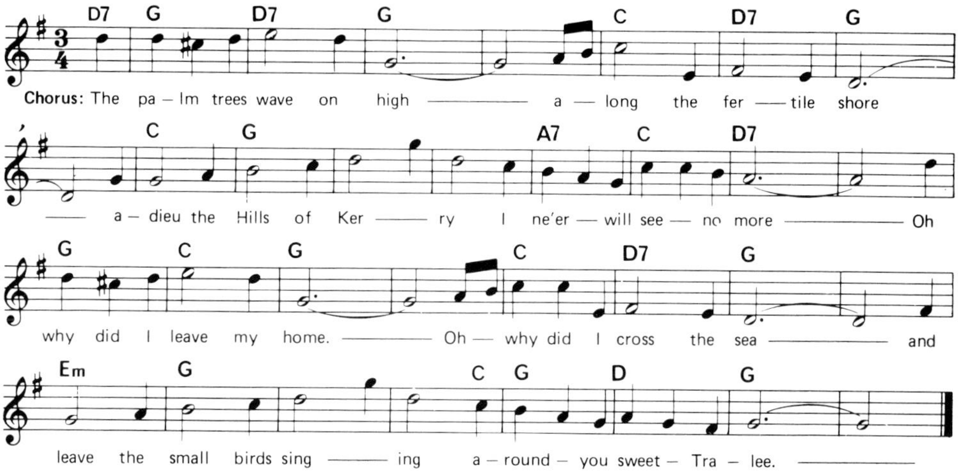

The noble and the brave have departed from our shore
They've gone off to a foreign land where the wild canyons roar
No more they'll see the shamrock, the plant so dear to me
Or hear the small birds singing around sweet Tralee.

Repeat Chorus:–

No more the sun will shine on that blessed harvest morn
Or hear our reaper singing in a golden field of corn
There's a band for every woe and a cure for every pain
But the happiness of my darling girl I never will see again.

Repeat Chorus:–

EVICTION SCENE
After the Famine of 1848 scenes like this were common

FOUR GREEN FIELDS

This song was written by Tommy Makem. The old woman in the song is Ireland, and her four sons are the Four Provinces: Ulster, Munster, Leinster and Connaught.

'Long time ago' said the fine old woman
'There was war and death, plundering and pillage
My children starved in mountain, valley and sea
And their wailing cries they shook the very heavens
My four green fields ran red with their blood' said she.

'What have I now' said the fine old woman
'What have I now' this proud old woman did say
'I have four green fields and one of them's in bondage
In strangers' hands who tried to take it from me
But my sons have sons as brave as were their fathers
My four green fields will bloom once again' said she.

THE STONE OUTSIDE DAN MURPHY'S DOOR

Cont.........

When our day's work was over we'd meet there,
In the winter or spring the same,
The boys and the girls all together,
Then would join in some innocent game.
Dan Murphy would bring down his fiddle,
While his daughters look'd after the store,
The music would ring, and sweet songs we would sing
On the stone outside Dan Murphy's door!

Chorus: –

Back again will our thoughts often wander,
To the scenes of our childhood's home
The friends and companions we left there,
It was poverty caused us to roam.
Since then in this life we have prospered;
But now still in our hearts we feel sure,
For mem'ry will fly to the days now gone by,
And the stone outside Dan Murphy's door!

Chorus: –

Published by WALTONS

THE GYPSY

You met me at the market
When your Ma was not with you
And you liked my long brown ringlets
And my handkerchief of blue
Although I'm very fond of you
And you asked me home to tea
I am a gypsy rover, love,
And you can't come with me.

Go home, girl, go home.

Your brother is a peeler
And he would put me in jail
If he knew I was a poacher
And I hunt your lord's best game
Your Daddy is a gentleman
Your Mammy is just as grand
But I'm a gypsy rover, love,
I'll not be your husband.

Go home, girl, go home.

The hours drawing on, love
And your Ma's expecting thee
Don't you tell her that you met me here
Or I'm a gypsy
Let's get off my jacket now
Your love will have to wait
For I am twenty-two years old
And you you're only eight.

Go home, girl, go home
Go home, girl, go home.

PATRICK WAS A GENTLEMAN

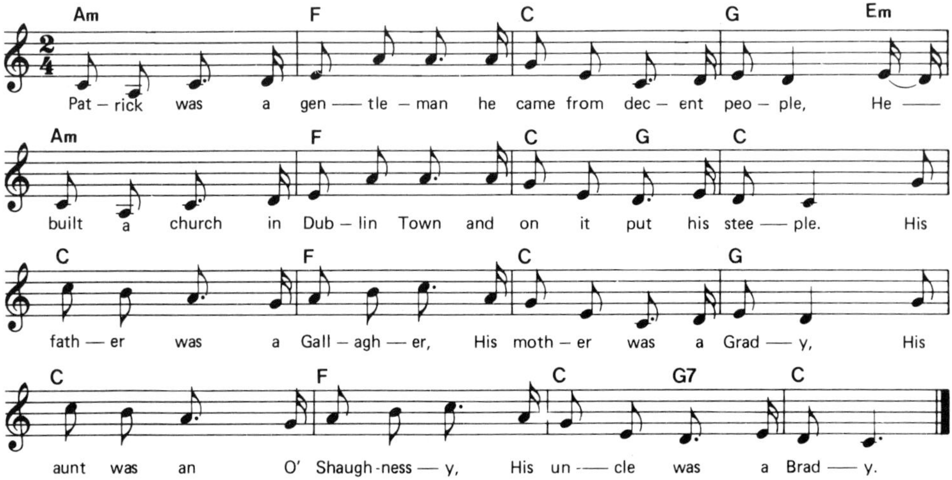

The Wicklow hills are very high, and so is the hill of Howth sir
But there's a hill much higher still, much higher than them both, sir.
On the top of this high hill St. Patrick preached his sermon
Which drove the frogs into the bogs, and banished all the vermin.
There's not a mile of Eireann's Isle where dirty vermin musters
But there he put his dear fore-foot and murdered them in clusters.
The frogs went hop and the toads went pop slapdash into the water
And the snakes committed suicide to save themselves from slaughter.

Nine hundred thousand reptiles blue he charmed with sweet discourses
And dined on them in Killaloe on soups and second courses.
Where blind worms crawling in the grass disgusted all the nation,
Right down to Hell with a holy spell he changed their situation.
No wonder that them Irish lads should be so gay and risky
Sure St. Pat he taught them that as well as making whiskey.

No wonder that the saint himself should understand distilling
For his mother kept a shebeen shop in the town of Enniskillen.
Was I but so fortunate as to be back in Munster,
I'd be bound that from that ground I never more would once stir.
There St. Patrick planted turf, cabbages and praties
Pigs galore, mo grá, mo stór, Altar boys and ladies.

This is a song about the production of illicit alcohol, (Poteen) and the attempt by the Excise Officers to control it.

THE HILLS OF CONNEMARA

Keep your eyes well peeled today; The tall, tall men are on their way
Searching for the mountain tay; In the hills of Connemara.

Swing to the left and swing to the right; The excise men will dance all night
Drinking up the tay till the broad daylight; In the hills of Connemara.

A gallon for the butcher, a quart for Tom; A bottle for poor old Father Tom
To help the poor old dear along; In the hills of Connemara.

Stand your ground, it is too late; The excise men are at the gate,
Glory be to Paddy but they're drinking it nate; In the hills of Connemara.

FAIR DAY, EYRE SQUARE, GALWAY
Eyre Square is now the city's main thoroughfare

THE TOWN OF BALLYBAY

Chorus:–

And she had a wooden leg that was hollow down the middle
She used to tie a string on it and play it like a fiddle
She fiddled in the hall, she fiddled in the alleyway
She didn't give a damn she had to fiddle anyway.

Chorus:–

And she said she couldn't dance unless she had her wellie on
But when she had it on she could dance as well as anyone
She wouldn't go to bed unless she had her shimmy on
But when she had it on she would go as quick as anyone.

Chorus:–

She had lovers by the score every Tom and Dick and Harry
She was courting night and day but still she wouldn't marry
And then she fell in love with a fella with a stammer
When he tried to run away she hit him with a hammer.

Chorus:–

She had childer up the stairs, she had childer in the brier
And another ten or twelve sitting roaring by the fire
She fed them on potatoes and on soup she made with nettles
And on lumps of hairy bacon that she boiled up in the kettle.

Chorus:–

So she led a sheltered life eating porridge and black pudding
And she terrorised her man until he died right sudden
And when the husband died she was feeling very sorry
She rolled him in a bag and she threw him in a quarry.

BIG STRONG MAN (Sylvest)

He thought he'd take a trip to Italy; He thought that he'd go by sea.
He dived off the harbour in New York; He swam like a great big shark.
He saw the Lusitania in distress; Put the Lusitania on his chest,
Drank all the water in the sea; He walked all the way to Italy.

Chorus:–

He thought he'd take a trip to old Japan; They brought out the big brass band,
He played every instrument they'd got; What a lad, he played the whole lot,
The old church bell will ring; The old church choir will sing,
They all turned out to say farewell, To my big brother Sylvest.

THE BOYS OF THE OLD BRIGADE

In hills and farms the call to arms was heard by one and all,
And from the glens came brave young men to answer Ireland's call.
'Twas long ago we faced the foe, the old brigade and me,
But by my side they fought and died that Ireland might be free.

Chorus:–

And now my boy I've told you why on Easter morn I sigh
For I recall my comrades all from dark old days gone by,
I think of men who fought in glens with rifles and grenade
May Heaven keep the men who sleep from the ranks of the old brigade.

Chorus:–

Published by WALTONS

DUBLIN JACK OF ALL TRADES

On George's Quay I first began and there became a porter
Me and my master soon fell out which cut my acquaintance shorter
In Sackville Street, a pastry cook; In James' Street, a baker
In Cook Street, I did coffins make; In Eustace Street, a preacher.

In Baggot Street I drove a cab and there was well requited
In Francis Street had lodging beds, to entertain all strangers
For Dublin is of high renown, or I am much mistaken
In Kevin Street, I do declare, sold butter, eggs and bacon.

In Golden Lane I sold old shoes; In Meath Street was a grinder
In Barrack Street I lost my wife, I'm glad I ne'er could find her
In Mary's Lane, I've dyed old clothes, of which I've often boasted
In that noted place Exchequer Street, sold mutton ready roasted.

In Temple Bar, I dressed old hats; In Thomas Street, a sawyer
In Pill Lane, I sold the plate, In Green Street, an honest lawyer
In Plunkett Street I sold cast clothes; In Bride's Alley, a broker
In Charles Street I had a shop, sold shovel, tongs and poker.

In College Green a banker was, and in Smithfield, a drover
In Britain Street, a waiter and in George's Street, a glover
On Ormond Quay I sold old books; In King Street, a nailer
In Townsend Street, a carpenter; And in Ringsend, a sailor.

Cont. ....

In Cole's Lane, a jobbing butcher; In Dame Street, a tailor
In Moore Street, a chandler and on the Coombe, a weaver.
In Church Street, I sold old ropes; On Redmond's Hill, a draper
In Mary Street, sold 'bacco pipes; In Bishop Street, a quaker.

In Peter Street, I was a quack; In Greek Street, a grainer
On the Harbour, I did carry sacks; In Werburgh Street, a glazier
In Mud Island, was a dairy boy, where I became a scooper
In Capel Street, a barber's clerk; In Abbey Street, a cooper.

In Liffey Street, had furniture with fleas and bugs I sold it
And at the Bank, a big placard, I often stood to hold it
In New Street I sold hay and straw, and in Spitalfields made bacon
In Fishamble Street was at the grand old trade of basketmaking.

In Summerhill, a coachmaker; In Denzille Street, a gilder
In Cork Street was a tanner; In Brunswick Street, a builder
In High Street, I sold hosiery; In Patrick Street, sold all blades
So if you wish to know my name; They call me Jack of all Trades.

GRAFTON STREET, DUBLIN

THE CRACK WAS NINETY IN THE ISLE OF MAN

Before we reached the Alexander Base; The ding dong we did surely raise,
In the bar of the ship we had great sport, as the boat she sailed out of the port.
Landed up in the Douglas Head; Enquired for a vacant bed.
The dining room we soon got shown by a decent woman up the road.
'Lads, ate it if you can, The crack was ninety in the Isle of Man.

Next morning we went for a ramble round; Viewed the sights of Douglas Town,
Then we went for a mighty session, in a pub they call Dick Darbies.
We must have been drunk by half-past three; To sober up we went swimmin' in the sea.
Back to the digs for the spruce up, and while waitin' for the fry
We all drew up our plan; The crack was ninety in the Isle of Man.

That night we went to the Texas Bar; Came back down by horse and car,
Met Big Jim and all went in to drink some wine in Yate's.
The Liverpool Judies it was said, were all to be found in the Douglas Head,
McShane was there in his suit and shirt, Them foreign girls he was tryin' to flirt,
Sayin' "Here girls, I'm your man," The crack was ninety in the Isle of Man.

Whacker fancied his good looks; On an Isle of Man woman he was struck.
But a Liverpool lad was by her side, And he throwin' the jar into her.
Whacker thought he'd take a chance; He asked the quare one out to dance,
Around the floor they stepped it out, And to Whack it was no bother.
Everythin' was goin' to plan; The crack was ninety in the Isle of Man.

The Isle of Man woman fancied Whack; Your man stood there till his mates came back
Whack! they all whacked into Whack, and Whack was whacked out on his back.
The police force arrived as well, Banjoed a couple of them as well,
Landed up in the Douglas jail, until the Dublin boat did sail,
Deported every man, The crack was ninety in the Isle of Man.

HENRY MY SON

It is believed by many that the tragic hero in this Ballad was Randolf, Earl of Leinster who died in 1232.

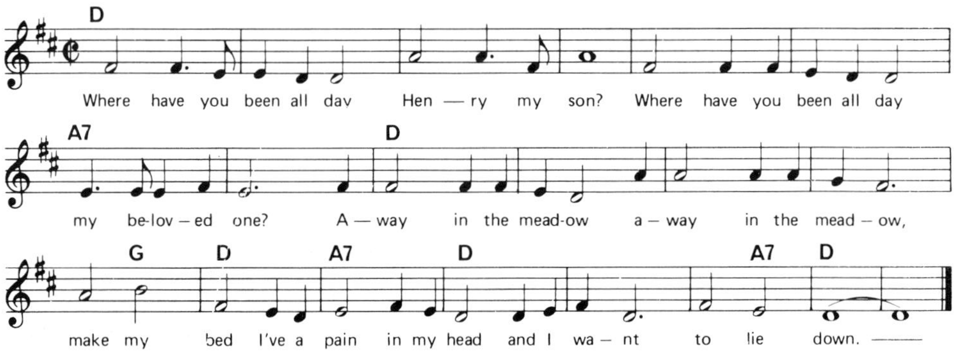

And what did you have to eat, Henry my son
What did you have to eat, my beloved one
Poison beads, poison beads
Make my bed I've a pain in my head and I want to lie down.

And what colour were them beads, Henry my son
What colour were them beads, my beloved one
Green an' yellow, green an' yellow
Make my bed I've a pain in my head and I want to lie down.

And what will you leave your mother, Henry my son
And what will you leave your mother, my beloved one
A woollen blanket, a woollen blanket
Make my bed I've a pain in my head and I want to lie down.

And what will you leave your children, Henry my son
And what will you leave your children, my beloved one
The keys of heaven, the keys of heaven
Make my bed I've a pain in my head and I want to lie down.

And what will you leave your sweetheart, Henry my son
And what will you leave your sweetheart, my beloved one
A rope to hang her, a rope to hang her
Make my bed I've a pain in my head and I want to lie down.

SONG FOR IRELAND

Talking all the day, with true friends who try to make you stay,
Telling jokes and news, singing songs to pass the night away.
Watched the Galway salmon run, like silver, dancing, darting in the sun.

Chorus:–

Drinking all the day, in old pubs where fiddlers love to play,
Saw one touch the bow, he played a reel which seemed so grand and gay.
Stood on Dingle beach and cast, in wild foam we found Atlantic bass.

Chorus:–

Dreaming in the night, I saw a land where no one has to fight,
Waking in your dawn, I saw you crying in the morning light.
Lying where the falcons fly, they twist and turn all in your air blue sky.

Chorus:–

Words & Music by PHIL COLCLOUGH

Published by MISTY RIVER MUSIC LTD

JOHNNY I HARDLY KNEW YE

This song constitutes a strong comment on the woes of war. The lyrics are thought to date from the 19th cent. while Patrick Gilmore is accredited with writing the tune

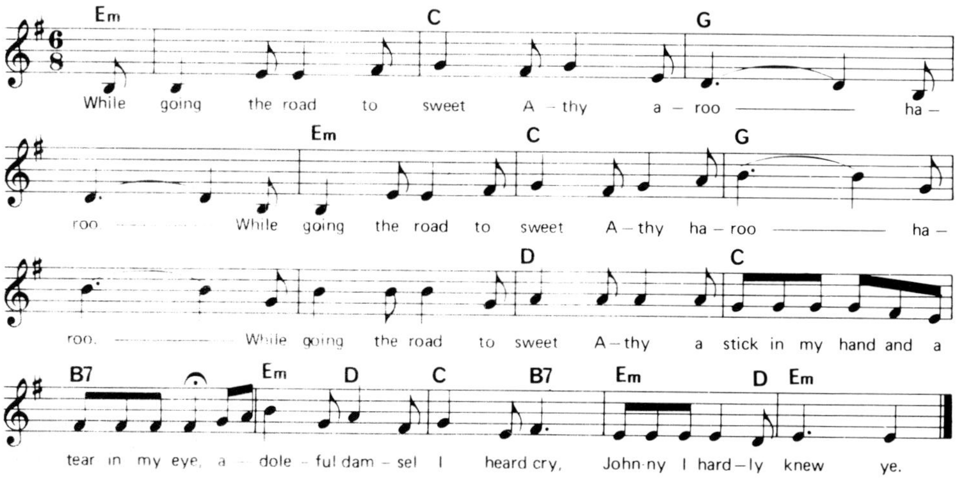

Chorus:–

With your drums and guns and guns and drums, A-roo, Ha-roo
With your drums and guns and guns and drums, A-roo, Ha-roo
With your drums and guns and guns and drums, the enemy nearly slew ye
My darling dear, you look so queer, Och, Johnny, I hardly knew ye!

Where are your eyes that looked so mild, A-roo, Ha-roo
Where are your eyes that looked so mild, A-roo, Ha-roo
Where are your eyes that looked so mild, when my poor heart you first beguiled
Why did you run from me and the child, Johnny, I hardly knew ye!

Chorus:–

Where are the legs with which you run, A-roo, Ha-roo
Where are the legs with which you run, A-roo, Ha-roo
Where are the legs with which you run, when you went to carry a gun?
Indeed your dancing days are done, Johnny, I hardly knew ye!

Chorus:–

It grieved my heart to see you sail, A-roo, Ha-roo
It grieved my heart to see you sail, A-roo, Ha-roo
It grieved my heart to see you sail, though from my heart you took leg bail
Like a cod you're doubled up head and tail, Johnny, I hardly knew ye!

Chorus:–

You haven't an arm and you haven't a leg, A-roo, Ha-roo
You haven't an arm and you haven't a leg, A-roo, Ha-roo
You haven't an arm and you haven't a leg, you're an eyeless, noseless, chickenless egg
You'll have to be put in a bowl to beg, Johnny, I hardly knew ye!

Chorus:–

I'm happy for to see you home, A-roo, Ha-roo
I'm happy for to see you home, A-roo, Ha-roo
I'm happy for to see you home, all from the Island of Sulloon
So low in flesh, so high in bone, Johnny, I hardly knew ye!

Chorus:–

But sad as it is to see you so, A-roo, Ha-roo
But sad as it is to see you so, A-roo, Ha-roo
But sad as it is to see you so, and I think of you now as an object of woe
Your Peggy'll still keep ye on as her beau, Johnny, I hardly knew ye!

Chorus:–

LEINSTER HOUSE, DUBLIN, (Published 1783)
Formerly the Duke of Leinster's Home

THE KERRY DANCES

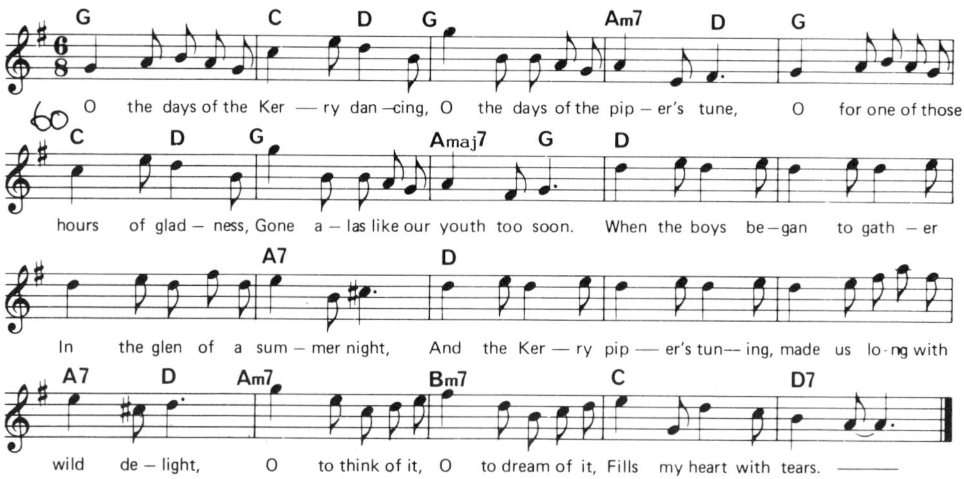

Was there ever a sweeter colleen in the dance than Eily More,
Or a prouder lad than Thady as he boldly took the floor.
"Lads and lassies, to your places, up the middle and down again",
And the merry hearted laughter ringing through the happy glen,
Oh to think of it, Oh to dream of it, fills my heart with tears.

O the days of the Kerry dancing, O the ring of the piper's tune,
O for one of those hours of gladness, Gone, alas like our youth too soon.

NEW YORK GIRLS (Can You Dance The Polka)

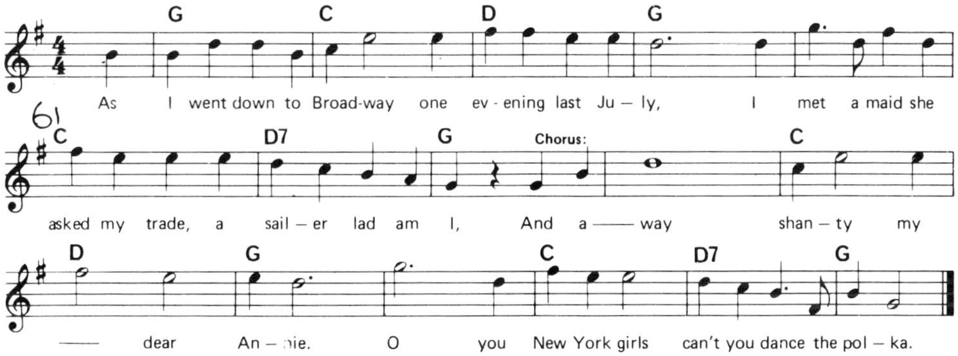

To Tiffiney's I took her I did not mind expense
I bought her a pair of gold ear-rings and they cost me 15 cents.

She said 'my fine new sailor now take me home you may'
But when we reached her cottage door she this to me did say,
'My flash man he's a Yankee with hair cut short behind
He wears a pair of tall sea boots and he sails in the black bow line.'

He's homeward bound this evening and with me he will stay
So get a move on sailor boy, get cracking on your way.

I kissed her hard and proper before her flash man came
Saying 'fare thee well me bowery girl I know your little game

I wrapped me glad rags round me and to the docks did steer
I'll never court another girl, I'll stick to rum and beer.

I joined a Yankee blood boat and sailed away next morn
Don't mess around with women lads you're safer round Cape Horn.

PADDY WORKS ON THE RAILWAY

This Ballad is also known as "Paddy works on the Erie" referring to the Erie Canal. Many Irishmen worked on the building of the American Transcontinental Railway.

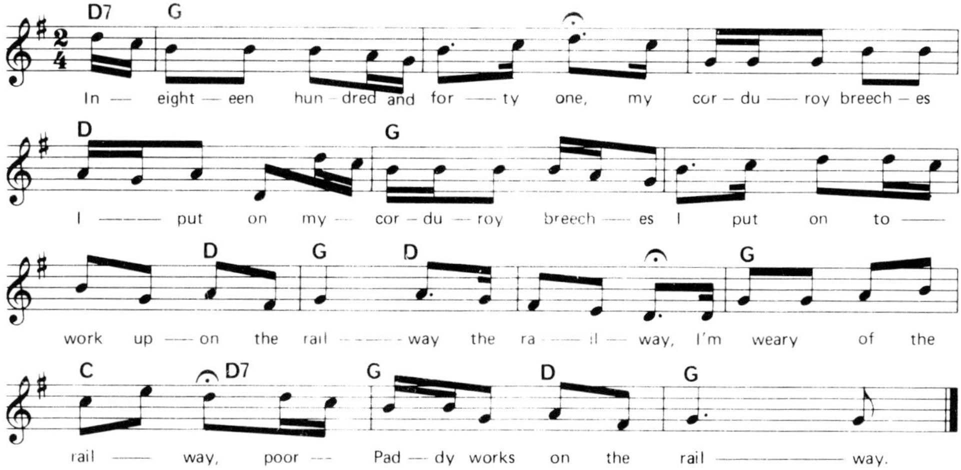

In eighteen hundred and forty two; I didn't know what I should do
I didn't know what I should do; To work upon the railway.

In eighteen hundred and forty three; I took a trip across the sea
I took a trip across the sea; To work upon the railway.

In eighteen hundred and forty four; I landed on Columbia's shore
I landed on Columbia's shore; To work upon the railway.

In eighteen hundred and forty five; When Daniel O'Connell was alive
When Daniel O'Connell was alive; To work upon the railway.

In eighteen hundred and forty six; I changed my trade to carrying bricks
I changed my trade to carrying bricks; To work upon the railway.

In eighteen hundred and forty seven; Poor Paddy was thinking of going to heaven
Poor Paddy was thinking of going to heaven; To work upon the railway.

In eighteen hundred and forty eight; I learnt to take my whiskey straight
I learnt to take my whiskey straight; To work upon the railway.

MUIRSHEEN DURKIN

A song given to us by Colm O'Loughlin. The tune was originally "Cailini Deas Mhuigheo" (The Beautiful Girls of Mayo)

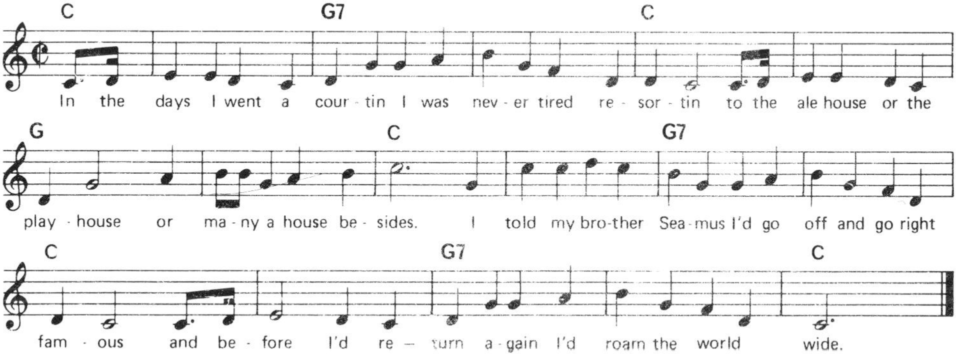

Chorus:–

So goodbye Muirsheen Durkin I'm sick and tired of working
No more I'll dig the praties, no longer I'll be fooled
As sure as me name is Carney, I'll go off to California,
Where instead of diggin' praties, I'll be diggin' lumps of gold.
I've courted girls in Blarney, in Kanturk and in Killarney
In Passage and in Queenstown, that is the Cobh of Cork
So goodbye to all this pleasure for I'm going to take me leisure
And the next time you will hear from me, will be a letter from New York.

Goodbye to all the boys at home, I'm sailing far across the foam
To try and make me fortune in far Amerikay; There's gold and money plenty
For the poor and for the gentry, And when I come back again I never more will stray.

Repeat Chorus:–

Published by THREE CANDLES MUSIC

QUEENSTOWN (COBH), CO. CORK
The emberkation point for emigrants to America.

MASTER McGRATH

This song tells the story of a great greyhound owned by Lord Lurgan, which won the Waterloo Cup in 1868, '69 and '71. The dog died of pneumonia during Christmas of 1871. There are two monuments to him in Co. Waterford.

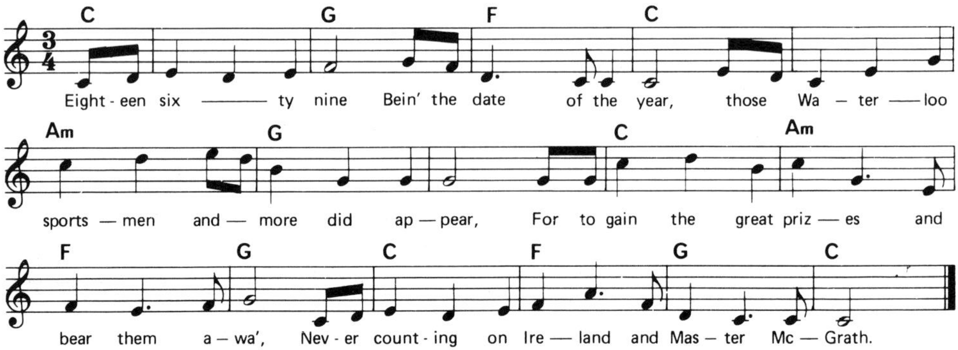

On the twelfth of November, that day of renown
McGrath and his keeper they left Lurgan town,
A gale in the channel, it soon drove them o'er,
On the thirteenth, they landed on England's fair shore.

Oh well, when they arrived in big London Town
Those great English "Sportsmen", they all gathered round
And one of those gentlemen standing nearby
Said, "Is that the great dog you call Master McGrath?"

Oh well, one of those gentlemen standing around
Says, "I don't care a damn for your Irish greyhound"
And another, he sneered with a scornful "Ha! Ha!
We'll soon humble the pride of your Master McGrath."

Then Lord Lurgan came forward and said, "Gentlemen,
If there's any amongst you has money to spend
For your grand English nobles I don't care a straw
Here's five thousand to one upon Master McGrath."

Oh McGrath he looked up and he wagged his old tail
Informing his lordship, 'Sure I know what you mane
Don't fear noble Brownlow, don't fear them agra
We'll soon tarnish their laurels," says Master McGrath.

Oh well Rose stood uncovered, the great English pride
Her master and keeper were close by her side
They let them away and the crowd cried "Hurrah"
For the pride of all England, and Master McGrath.

Oh well Rose and the Master, they both ran along
"I wonder" says Rose, "what took you from your home
You should have stayed there in your Irish domain,
And not come to gain laurels on Albion's plain".

"Well, I know," says the Master, "we have wild heather bogs
But, bedad, in old Ireland there's good men and dogs
Lead on, bold Britannia, give none of your jaw
Stuff that up your nostrils," says Master McGrath.

Well the hare she led on just as swift as the wind
He was sometimes before her and sometimes behind
He jumped on her back and held up his ould paw
"Long live the Republic", says Master McGrath.

THE MOONSHINER

I'll go to some hollow in this counterie,
Ten gallons of wash I can go on the spree,
No woman to follow and the world is all mine,
I love none so well as I love the moonshine.

Chorus:–

Moonshine, dear moonshine, oh! how I love thee,
You kill'd my poor father, but dare you try me.
Bless all moonshiners and bless all moonshine,
Its breath smells as sweet as the dew on the vine.

Chorus:–

I'll have moonshine for Liza and moonshine for May,
Moonshine for Lu and she'll sing all the day,
Moonshine for my breakfast, moonshine for my tea,
Moonshine, my hearties, it's moonshine for me.

Chorus:–

O'SULLIVAN'S JOHN

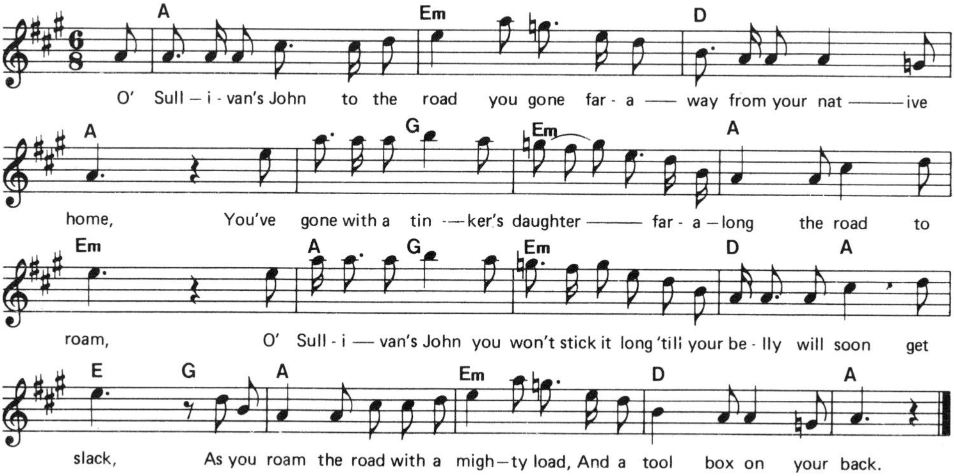

O Sullivan's John to the road you've gone, far away from your native home
You've gone with a tinker's daughter far, along the road to roam.
O Sullivan's John you won't stick it long, 'till your belly will soon get slack
As you roam the road with a mighty load, and a tool-box on your back.

I met Katie Coffey with her neat baby behind on her back strapped on,
She'd an old ash plant in her hand for to drive her donkey on.
Enquiring at every farmer's house as along the road she passed
And it's where would she get an old pot to mend or where would she get an ass.

There's a hairy ass there in the County Clare in a place they call Spancel-hill
Where my brother James got a wrap of a haimes and poor Paddy they tried to kill
They loaded him up on an ass and cart while Kate and big Mary looked on
Ah, bad luck to the day that I went away to join with the tinker's band.

Repeat first verse again ....

Published by BELWIN MILLS MUSIC LTD

This song was written in the early part of this century and originated in County Cork. Thady Quill is rum–oured to have lived in the Mushra Mountains near Macroom, Co. Cork.

BOLD THADY QUILL

Chorus:–

For rambling or bowling, for football or coursing
For emptying a bowl just as fast as you'd fill
In all your days roving you'll find none so jovial
As the Muskerry sportsman, the bould Thady Quill.

At the great hurling match between Cork and Tipperary
'Twas played in the Park, on the banks of the Lee
Our own darling boys were afraid of being beaten
So they sent for bould Thady to Ballinagree
He hurled the ball right and left in their faces
And showed the Tipperary boys action and skill
If they touched on our lines he did manfully brave them
And they put in the paper the praise of Thady Quill.

Repeat Chorus:–

Cont..........

Our Thady is famous in a great many places
At the athletic races held down in Cloughroe
He won the long jump without throwing off his waistcoat
Going twenty-four feet from the heel to the toe
And at throwing the weight, with Dublinman foremost
Our own darling Thady, exceeded him still
And all round the field went the loud swinging chorus
Long life and success to the bould Thady Quill.

Repeat Chorus:–

At the Cork Exhibition there was a fair lady
Her fortune exceeded a million or more
But a bad constitution had ruined her completely
And medical treatment had failed o'er and o'er
Yerrah, mamma, says she, sure I know what will heal me
And cure the disease that is certain to kill
Give over your doctors and medical treatment
Let me have a stroll out with bould Thady Quill.

Repeat Chorus:–

Published by WALTONS

AN IRISH SHILLELAGH SELLER "Buy A Stick, yer Honer"

THE LARK IN THE MORNING

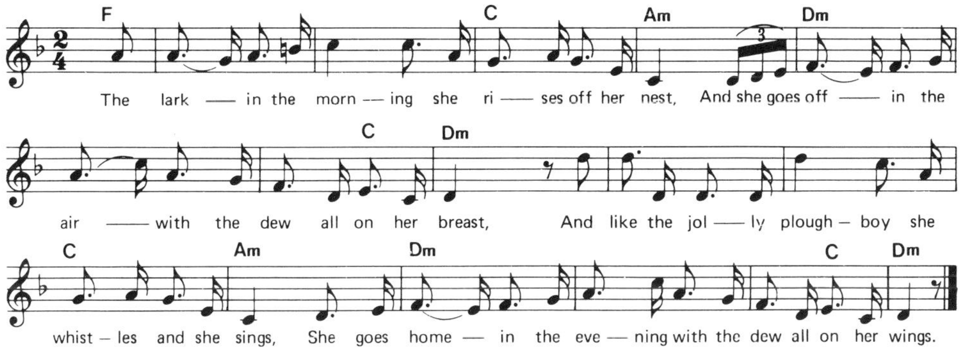

Oh, Roger the ploughboy he is a dashing blade,
He goes whistling and singing for yonder leafy shade
He met with dark-eyed Susan, she's handsome I declare,
And she is far more enticing than the birds all in the air.

As they were coming home from the rakes of the town,
The meadow bein' all mown and the grass had been cut down.
As they should chance to tumble all on the new-mown hay
Oh, it's kiss me now or never, this bonnie lass would say.

When twenty long weeks were over and past
Her mammy asked the reason why she thickened round the waist
'It was the pretty ploughboy' this girl then did say,
For he asked me for to tumble all on the new-mown hay

Here's a health to you ploughboys where ever you may be,
That like to have a bonnie lass a-sittin' on each knee.
With a pint of good strong porter he'll whistle and he'll sing
And the ploughboy is as happy as a prince or a king.

ENNISKILLEN, CO. FERMANAGH
Viewed from Portora side. Pub. Oct. 1778

O'DONNELL ABÚ

Princely O'Neill to our aid is advancing
With many a chieftain and warrior clan.
A thousand proud steeds in his vanguard are prancing
'Neath the borderers brave from the banks of the Bann.
Many a heart shall quail under its coat of mail,
Deeply the merciless foeman shall rue,
When on his ear shall ring, borne on the breeze's wing,
Tir Connell's dread war cry, "O'Donnell Abú!"

Wildly o'er Desmond the war wolf is howling;.
Fearless the eagle sweeps over the plain.
The fox in the streets of the city is prowling,
And all who would scare them are banished or slain.
On with O'Donnell, then, fight the old fight again;
Sons of Tir Connell, are valiant and true.
Make the proud Saxon feel Erin's avenging steel;
Strike for your country, O'Donnell Abú!

AS I ROVED OUT

Her boots were black and her
stockings white,
And her buckles shone like silver;
She had a dark and a rolling eye,
And her ear-rings tipped her shoulders.

"What age are you, my nice sweet girl?
What age are you, my honey?"
How modestly she answered me,
"I'll be sixteen age on Sunday."

Chorus:–

I went to the house on the top of the hill
When the moon was shining clearly;
She arose to let me in,
For her mammy chanced to hear her.

Chorus:–

She caught her by the hair of the head,
And down to the room she brought her;
And with the root of a hazel twig,
She was the well-beat daughter.

Chorus:–

"Will you marry me now, my soldier lad?
Marry me now or never?
Will you marry me now, my soldier lad,
For you see I'm done forever?"

Chorus:–

"No, I won't marry you, my bonny wee girl,
I won't marry you, my honey,
For I have got a wife at home,
And how could I disown her?"

Chorus:–

A pint a night is my delight,
And a gallon in the morning;
The old women are my heartbreak,
But the young ones are my darlings.

Chorus:–

THREE DRUNKEN MAIDENS

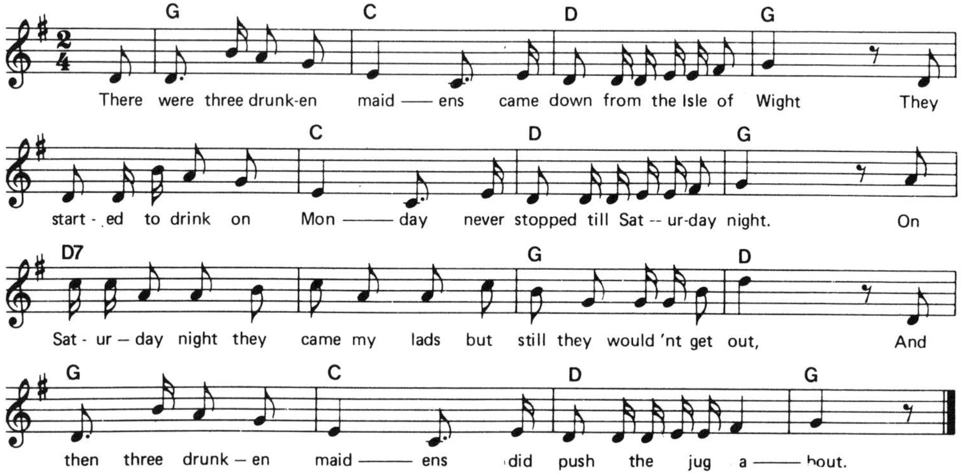

Then in came dancing Sally her cheeks a rosy bloom
Shove o'er you jolly sisters and give young Sal some room
And I will be your equal before the evening's out
And then three drunken maidens they pushed the jug about.

They had woodcock and pheasant, partridge and hare
And every sort of dainty, no shortage there was there
They'd forty gallons of beer me lads but still they wouldn't get out
And then three drunken maidens they pushed the jug about.

Then in came the landlord, he was looking for his pay
Forty pounds for beer me lads these girls were forced to pay
They had ten pounds a piece me lads but still they wouldn't get out
And then three drunken maidens they pushed the jug about.

Where are your fancy hats and your mantles rich and fine
They've all been swallowed up me lads with tankards of fine wine
And where are your fancy men, young maidens frisk and gay
You left them in the ale house and it's there you'll have to pay.

THE MAN FROM MULLINGAR

Oh! seven hundred peelers couldn't catch him – catch him
The king sent out an order for to lash him – lash him
When Patrick came to Dublin Town he stole an armoured car
And he gave it to the I.R.A. Brigade in Mullingar.

On Easter Monday morning when the boys declared a sound
Patrick raised the flag of war down in his native town
First he went to make his peace with dear old Father Maher
He went out and blew the barracks up and the man from Mullingar.

And when Ireland takes her place among the nations of the world
A flag of orange, white and green to the forewinds is unfurled
You'll read the role of honour and you'll find with a marked scar
The name of Sarsfield Mulligan, the Man from Mullingar.

JOSEPH BAKER

He'd rise up every morning before the break of day
And into the shady forest he'd go in pursuit of the royal deer.
He chased the wind right up the road and the water down the hill
He chased the breeze across the fields and the water to the mill.

Now sportsmen came from far and near to challenge Baker's speed,
In every race, in every place they swore they'd do the deed.
A Baker came from Birkenhead and a Sailor came from Mail,
A Butcher came from Yarmouth town and a Soldier came from Sale.

But he could not be beaten until that final day,
When death bestowed upon him and took his breath away.
So if you go out on a winter's night you'll see him running still,
His ghost runs down by Censley Church, right across to Caroup Hill.

Repeat first Verse:–

MY LOVELY ROSE OF CLARE

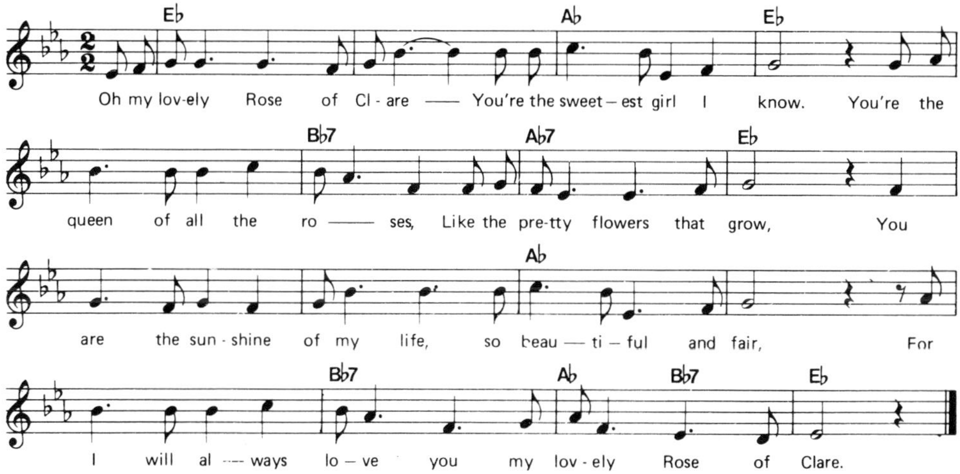

Chorus:–

We walked down by the river bank, watched the Shannon flowing by,
And listened to the nightingale singing songs for you and I.
And to say farewell to all you true and fair,
For I have stolen the heart of one, my lovely Rose of Clare.

Chorus:–

Published by VELVET MUSIC

THE BANKS OF RED ROSES

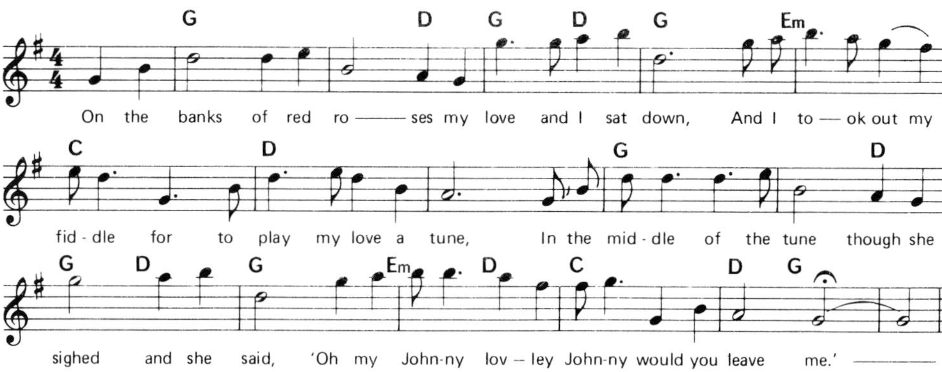

When I was a young girl I heard my mother say
That I was a foolish lass and easily led astray,
And before I would work I would sooner sport and play
With my Johnny on the Banks of Red Roses.

Well he took her to his lodge and he treated her to tea
Saying 'drink me dearest Mary and come along with me,'
Saying 'drink me dearest Mary and come along with me
To the sweet and lovely Banks of Red Roses.'

Well they walked and they talked till they came unto a cave
Where Johnny all the day had been digging up a grave
Where Johnny all the day had been digging up a grave
For to leave his lassie low among the Roses.

Well he took out a pen-knife it was both long and sharp
And he plunged it right into his own dear Mary's heart
And he plunged it right into his own dear Mary's heart
And he left her lying low among the Roses.

Daylight peeping through the curtains of
The passing night time is your smile
The sun in the sky is like your laugh
Come back to me Nancy linger for just a little while
Since you left these shores I know no peace nor joy.

Chorus:–

On the day in Spring when the snow starts to melt and streams to flow
With the birds I'll sing to you a song.
In the while I'll wander down by bluebell grove
Where wild flowers grow
And I'll hope that lovely Nancy will return.

Chorus:–

Published by MILD MUSIC LTD

FROM CLARE TO HERE

When Friday night comes around and he's only in the fighting
My ma would like a letter home but I'm too tired for writing.

Chorus:–

And the only time I feel alright is when I'm into drinking
It eases off the pain a bit and levels out my thinking.

Chorus:–

Well it almost breaks my heart when I think of Josephine
I promised I'd be coming back with pockets full of green.

Chorus:–

I dream I hear a piper play maybe it's a notion
I dream I see white horses dance upon that other ocean.

Chorus:–

Words & Music by RALPH McTELL
Published by MISTY RIVER MUSIC LTD

The song was written by Father P. O'Neill in tribute to the men who fought and died in the Easter Rising of 1916 in Dublin.

THE FOGGY DEW

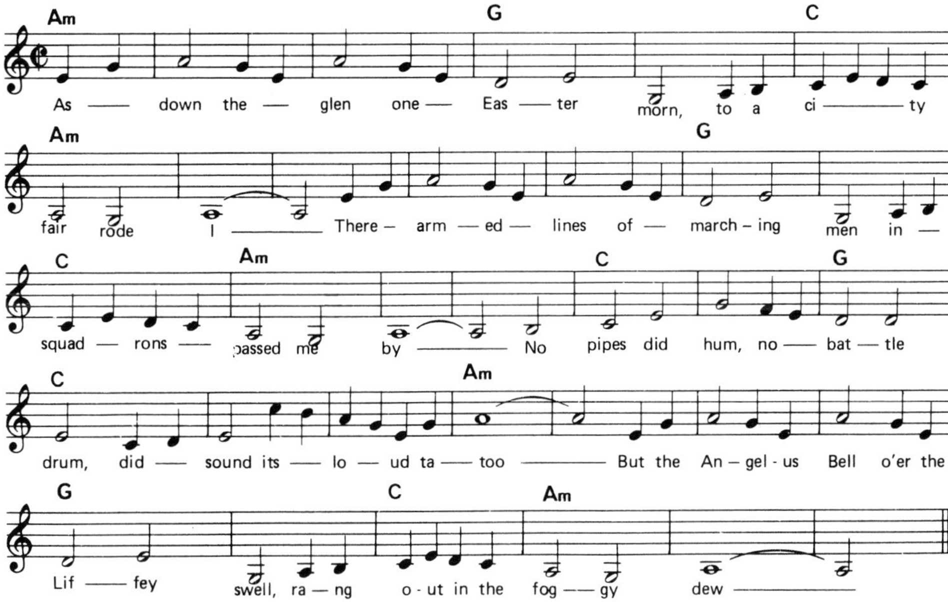

Right proudly high in Dublin Town they flung out the flag of war
'Twas better to die 'neath an Irish sky than at Suvla or Sud El Bar;
And from the plains of Royal Meath strong men came hurrying through
While Britannia's huns with their great big guns, sailed in through the Foggy Dew.

O the night fell black and the rifles' crack made "Perfidious Abion" reel
'Mid the leaden rail, seven tongues of flame did shine o'er the lines of steel;
By each shining blade, a prayer was said that to Ireland her sons be true
And when morning broke still the war flag shook out its fold in the Foggy Dew.

'Twas England bade our Wild Geese go that small nations might be free
But their lonely graves are by Suvla's waves or the fringe of the Great North Sea
O had they died by Pearse's side, or had fought with Cathal Brugha
Their names we'd keep where the Fenians sleep, 'neath the shroud of the Foggy Dew.

But the bravest fell, and the requiem bell rang mournfully and clear
For those who died that watertide in the springtime of the year
While the world did gaze, with deep amaze, at those fearless men, but few
Who bore the fight that Freedom's light might shine through the Foggy Dew.

Ah, back through the glen I rode again, and my heart with grief was sore
For I parted then with valiant men whom I never shall see more
But to and fro in my dreams I go and I'd kneel and pray for you
For slavery fled, O glorious dead, when you fell in the Foggy Dew.

MRS. McGRATH

This was a popular marching song in Ireland during the years leading up to the Easter Rebellion of 1916. Ironically it is a very evocative anti-war song

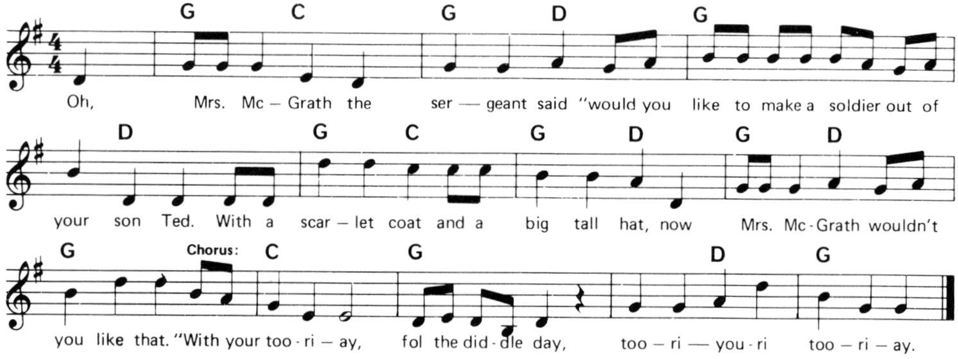

Now Mrs. McGrath lived on the sea-shore, for the space of seven long years or more
Till she saw a big ship sailing into the bay, "Here's my son Ted, will ye clear the way".

Repeat Chorus:–

"Oh, Captain dear, where have you been; Have you been in the Mediterreen?
Will you tell me the news of my son Ted, is the poor boy living or is he dead?"

Repeat Chorus:–

Ah well up comes Ted without any legs, and in their place he had two wooden pegs
Well she kissed him a dozen times or two, saying "Glory be to God, shure it wouldn't be you!

Repeat Chorus:–

"Oh then were ye drunk, or were ye blind, that ye left your two fine legs behind?
Or was it while walking on the sea, a big fish ate yer legs from the knees away?"

Repeat Chorus:–

"Well I wasn't drunk and I wasn't blind, when I left my two fine legs behind
But a cannon ball on the fifth of May, tore my two fine legs from the knees away".

Repeat Chorus:–

"Oh, Teddy me boy," the old widow cried, "Yer two fine legs were yer mammy's pride
Them stumps of a tree wouldn't do at all, Why didn't you run from the big cannon ball?"

Repeat Chorus:–

"Well all foreign wars I do proclaim, between Don John and the King of Spain
And by herrins I'll make them rue the time, that they swept the legs from a child of mine".

TRI–COLOURED RIBBON

He whispered, "Good-bye love, old Ireland is calling,
High over Dublin our Tri-colour flies,
In the streets of the City the foe man is falling,
And wee birds are singing 'Old Ireland arise'."

His bandolier around him, his bright bayonet shining,
His short service rifle, a beauty to see,
There was joy in his eyes, though he left me repining,
And started away for to make Ireland free.

In prayer and in watching the dark days passed over,
The roar of the guns brought no message to me.
I prayed for Old Ireland, I prayed for my true love,
That he might be safe, and Old Ireland be free.

The struggle has ended, they brought me the story,
The last whispered message he sent unto me,
"I was true to my land, love; I fought for her glory,
And gave up my life for to make Ireland free."

Published by WALTONS

THE RAGGLE–TAGGLE GYPSY

This song, although popular in Ireland is of Scottish origin. The song tells of a lady living in comfort and leisure who absconds with the gypsies. The event is thought to have been an actual one.

Then she pulled off her silk finished gown; And put on a hose of leather–o
The ragged ragged rags about our door; She is gone with the raggle-taggle gypsy–o.

It was late last night when my lord came home; Enquiring for his lady–o
The servants said on every hand; She is gone with the raggle-taggle gypsy–o.

O saddle for me my milk white steed; And go fetch me my pony–o
That I may go and seek my bride; Who is gone with the raggle-taggle gypsy–o.

O he rode high and he rode low; He rode through wood and copses–o
Until he came to a wide open field; And there he spied his lady–o.

O what made you leave your house and land; What made you leave your money–o
What made you leave your new-wedded lord; To be off with the raggle-taggle gypsy–o.

O what care I for my house and land; What care I for money–o
What care I for my new-wedded lord; I'm off with the raggle-taggle gypsy–o.

Last night you slept on a goose feathered bed; With the sheet turned down so bravely–o
Tonight you'll sleep in a cold open field; Along with the raggle-taggle gypsy–o.

O what care I for my goose feathered bed; With the sheet turned down so bravely–o
Tonight I will sleep in a cold open field; Along with the raggle-taggle gypsy–o.

THE LITTLE BEGGARMAN

I slept last night
In a barn at Currabawn
A wet night came on
And I slipped through the door
Holes in me shoes
And the toes peepin' through
Singin' skiddy-me-re-me-doodlum
For ould Johnnie Dhu.

Chorus:

I must be gettin' home
For it's gettin' late at night
The fire's all raked
And there isn't any light
And now you've heard me story
Of the old ricadoo
It's good-night and God bless you
From ould Johnnie Dhu.

Chorus:

THE PORTICO OF THE PARLIAMENT HOUSE (now the Bank of Ireland, College Green). Pub. Dec. 1795

SALLY BROWN

Miss Sally Brown she's a nice young lady, Way hay roll on board
Oh we rolled all night rolled till the day, Gonna spend my money on Sally Brown.

Her mammy doesn't like a tarry sailor, Way hay roll on board,
Oh we rolled all night rolled till the day, Gonna spend my money on Sally Brown.

She wants her to marry a one legged Captain, Way hay roll on board,
Oh we rolled all night rolled till the day, Gonna spend my money on Sally Brown.

A song to celebrate the "hauling home", i.e. the return of groom to his house with his bride. This usually took place one month after the wedding.

ÓRÓ 'SÉ DO BHEATHA 'BHAILE

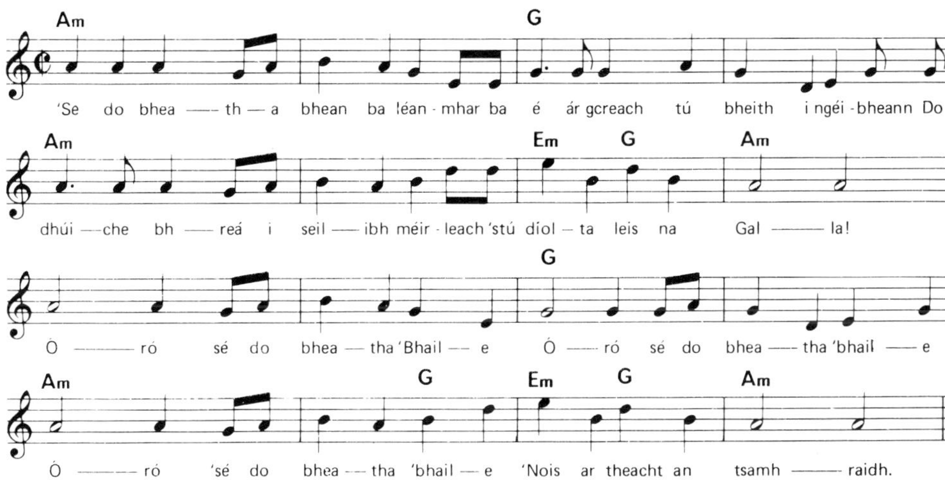

Tá Gráinne Mhaol ag teacht thar sàile; Óglaigh armtha léi mar gharda
Gaeil iad féin is ní Gaill ná Spáinnigh; Is cuirfidh siad ruaig ar Ghallaibh.

Repeat Chorus:–

A bhuí le Ri na bhfeart go bhfeiceann; Muna mbíonn beo ina dheoidh ach seachtain
Gráinne Mhaol is míle gaiscíoch; Ag fógairt fáin ar Ghallaibh.

Repeat Chorus:–

FISH AND VEGETABLE WOMEN

HIGHLAND PADDY

In the mornin' we rose early
Just before the break of dawn
Blackbirds singing in the bushes
Greetings to a smiling morn.
Gather 'round me men of Ireland
Gather Fenians gather round
Hand to hand with sword and musket
Spill the blood upon this holy ground.

Chorus:–

There's a glen beside the river
Just outside Kilkenny Town
There we met this noble captain
Men lay dead upon the ground.

Chorus:–

There's a grave beside the river
A mile outside Kilkenny Town
There we laid our noble captain
Birds were silent when this Fenian died.
All my life I will remember
I'll remember night and day
That once I rode into Kilkenny
And I heard this noble captain say.

Chorus:–

DAN O'HARA

In the year of sixty four, I had acres by the score
And the grandest land you ever ran a plough through.
But the land-lord came you know and he laid our old home low,
So it's here I am to-day your broken-hearted.

Chorus:–

For twenty years or more did misfortune cross our door
And my poor old wife and I were sadly parted.
We were scattered far and wide and our children starved and died,
So it's here I am to-day your broken-hearted.

Chorus:–

Tho' in frost and snow I stand sure the shadow of God's hand
It lies warm about the brow of Dan O'Hara,
And soon with God above I will meet the ones I love,
And I'll find the joys I lost in Connemara.

Chorus:–

Published by WALTONS

THE MAID OF THE SWEET BROWN KNOWE

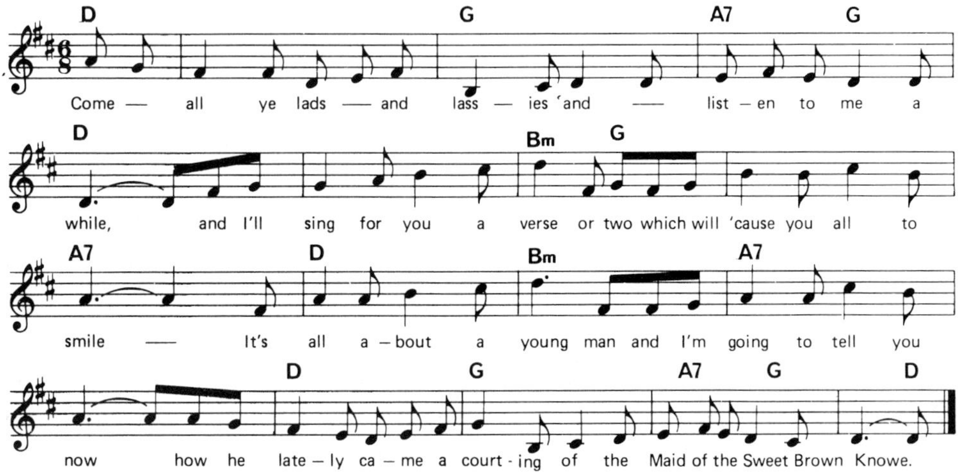

Said he, "My pretty fair maid, will you come along with me
We'll both go off together, and married we will be
We'll join our hands in wedlock bands, I'm speaking to you now
And I'll do my best endeavour for the Maid of the Sweet Brown Knowe."

Said he, "My pretty fair maid, how can you say so
Look down on yonder valley, where my crops do gently grow
Look down on yonder valley, where my horses and my plough
Are at their daily labour for the Maid of the Sweet Brown Knowe."

"If they're at their daily labour, kind sir, it's not for me
For I've heard of your behaviour, I have, indeed, " said she
"There is an inn where you call in, I have heard the people say
When you rap and call and pay for all, and go home at the break of day."

"If I rap and call and pay for all, the money is all my own
And I'll never spend your fortune, for I hear you have got none
You thought you had my poor heart broke in talking with me now
But I'll leave you where I found you, at the foot of the Sweet Brown Knowe."

This song was probably written in the 19th century. It is a lively and popular Ballad sung very quickly.

THE ROCKY ROAD TO DUBLIN

In Mullingar that night I rested limbs so weary
Started by daylight next morning light and airy
Took a drop of the pure, to keep me heart from sinking
That's an Irishman's cure, when e'er he's on for drinking
To see the lassies smile, laughing all the while
At my daring style, 'twould set your heart-a-bubblin'
Till I was almost tired of the rocky road to Dublin.

In Dublin next arrived, I thought it such a pity
To be so soon deprived a view of that fine city
When I took a stroll all among the quality
My bundle it was stole in that neat locality
Something crossed my mind, then I looked behind
No bundle I could find upon my stick a-wobblin'
Enquirin' for the rogue, they said my Connaught brogue
Wasn't much in vogue on the rocky road to Dublin.

Cont......

From there I got away, my spirits never failin'
Landed on the Quay as the ship was sailin'
Captain at me roared, said that no room had he
When I jumped aboard, a cabin found for Paddy
Down among the pigs, I played some funny rigs
Danced some hearty jigs, the water round me bubblin'
When off Holyhead I wished myself was dead
Or better far instead, on the rocky road to Dublin.

The boys of Liverpool, when we safely landed
Called meself the fool, I could no longer stand it
Blood began to boil, temper I was losin'
Poor old Erin's Isle they began abusin'
Hurrah me soul said I, me shillelagh I let fly
Some Galway boys came by, they saw I was a hobblin'
With a loud hurray, they joined in the affray
And quickly cleared the way for the rocky road to Dublin.

SOUTH GREAT GEORGES STREET, DUBLIN

THE HUMOUR IS ON ME NOW

Ah, be quiet you foolish daughter and hold your simple tongue,
You're better free and single and happy while you're young,
But the daughter shook her shoulders and milked her patient cow
Saying "I will and I must get married for the humour is on me now".

And, sure who are you to turn me, that married young yourself,
And took my darling mother from off the single shelf?
Ah, sure, daughter dear go aisy and milk your patient cow
For a man may have his humour but the humour is off me now.

Well indeed, I'll tell my mother the awful things you say,
Indeed I'll tell my mother this very blessed day;
Och, now, daughter have a heart, dear, you'll start a fearful row,
So I will unless I marry for the humour is on me now.

Och, if you must be married will you tell me who's the man,
And quickly she did answer there's William, James and John,
A carpenter, a tailor, and a man to milk the cow,
For I will and I must get married and the humour is on me now.

A carpenter's sharp a man, and tailor's hard to face,
With his legs across the table and his threads about the place,
And sure John's a fearful tyrant and never lacks a row–
But I will and I must be married for the humour is on me now.

Well if you must be married will you tell me what you'll do,
"Sure I will" the daughter answered, "Just the same as ma and you"
"I'll be mistress of my dairy and my butter and my cow",
"And your husband too, I'll venture, for the humour is on you now.

So, at last the daughter married and married well-to-do,
And loved her darling husband for a month, a year or two;
But John was all a tyrant and she quickly rued her vow
Saying "I'm sorry that I married for the humour is *off* me now".

IF YOU'RE IRISH COME INTO THE PARLOUR

Patrick loved the girl he wed,
But he could not stand his Ma-in-law,
Once with joy he turned quite red,
When she got into trouble thro' her jaw.
Six police they had, to take her to the court,
She was informed a month she would have to do,
So Patrick quickly wrote
Up to the Judge, a note,
Explaining, Sir, I'm much obliged to you!

Chorus:–

Words & Music by SHAUN GLENVILLE & FRANK MILLER

THE CASTLE OF DROMORE

Bring no ill wind to hinder us, my helpless babe and me
Dread spirit of Blackwater banks, Clan Eoin's wild banshee,
And Holy Mary pitying, in heaven for grace doth sue,
Sing hushabye, lul, lul, lo, lo, lan; Sing hushabye, lul, lul, loo.

Take time to thrive, my Rose of hope, in the garden of Dromore,
Take heed young Eagle – till your wings are weathered fit to soar;
A little time and then our land is full of things to do.
Sing hushabye, lul, lul, lo, lo, lan; Sing hushabye, lul, lul, loo.

THE COTTAGE BY THE LEE

'Tis grand to stand outside that cottage doorway,
And gaze across the cornfields rich and gold,
To hear the stream go rippling by the meadow,
Or watch the shepherd calling to his fold.
From down the lane, that winds behind the garden,
The black-bird greets the smiling summer morn,
And as his music echoes o'er the valley,
You smile and bless the day that you were born.
Yes that's my dream, my lovely dream of homeland,
And tho' I thought a rover I could be,
It's soon I found I left my heart behind me,
Within that lovely Cottage by the Lee.

Published by WALTONS

WHEN YOU WERE SWEET SIXTEEN

I love you as I've never loved before
Since first I saw you on the village green,
Come to me e'er my dreams of love are o'er
I love you as I loved you when you were sweet,
When you were sweet sixteen.

SAM HALL

This song was written by an English man, C. Ross. It deals with a chimney sweep who was hanged for burglary in 1701.

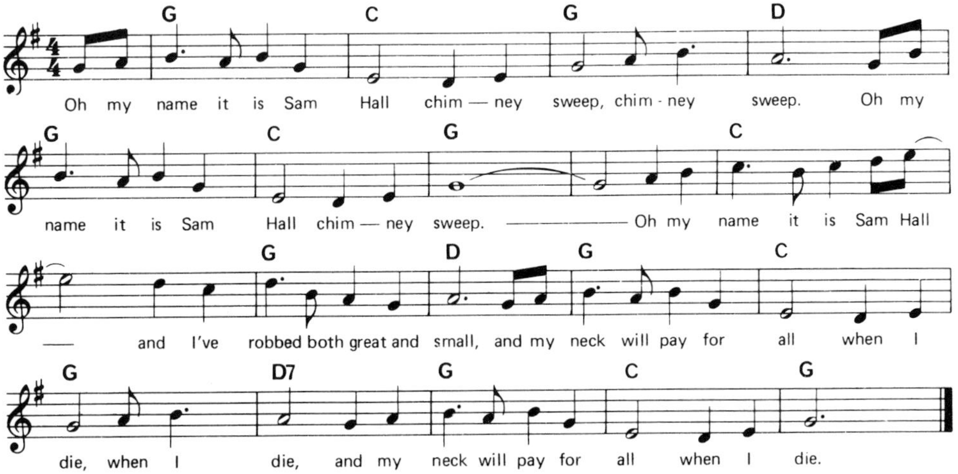

Oh they took me to Cootehill in a cart, in a cart
Oh they took me to Cootehill in a cart
Oh they took me to Cootehill and 'twas there I made my will
For the best of friends must part, so must I, so must I
For the best of friends must part, so must I.

Up the ladder I did grope, that's no joke, that's no joke
Up the ladder I did grope, that's no joke
Up the ladder I did grope and the hangman pulled his rope
And ne'er a word I spoke, tumbling down, tumbling down
And ne'er a word I spoke tumbling down.

(Repeat first Verse)

STRAWBERRY BEDS, CHAPELIZOD, DUBLIN
Near the Phoenix Park

THE RARE OULD TIMES

My name it is Sean Dempsey, as Dublin as can be
Born hard and late in Pimlico, in a house that ceased to be.
By trade I was a cooper, lost out to redundancy,
Like my house that fell to progress, my trade's a memory.
And I courted Peggy Dignan, as pretty as you please,
A rogue and a Child of Mary, from the rebel Liberties.
I lost her to a student chap, with skin as black as coal,
When he took her off to Birmingham, she took away my soul.

Chorus:–

The years have made me bitter, the gargle dims my brain,
'Cause Dublin keeps on changing, and nothing seems the same.
The Pillar and the Met. have gone, the Royal long since pulled down
As the great unyielding concrete, makes a city of my town.

Chorus:–

Fare thee well sweet Anna Liffey, I can no longer stay,
And watch the new glass cages, that spring up along the Quay.
My mind's too full of memories, to old to hear new chimes,
I'm part of what was Dublin, in the rare ould times.

Chorus:–

Words & Music PETE ST JOHN

Published by PETE ST JOHN/CELTIC SONGS/EMMA MUSIC

THE ROSE OF ALLENDALE

Where'er I wandered, east or west; Tho' fate began to lour
A solace still she was to me; In sorrow's lonely hour.
When tempests lashed our lonely barque; And rent her shiv'ring sail
One maiden form withstood the storm; 'Twas the Rose of Allendale.

And when my fever'd lips were parched on Afric's burning sands,
She whispered hopes of happiness, and tales of distant lands.
My life has been a wilderness, unblest by fortune's gale,
Had fate not linked my lot to hers, The Rose of Allendale.

Words & Music by RICHARD FARRELLY

ISLE OF INNISFREE

And when the moonlight peeps across the rooftops
Of this great city wondrous though it be
I scarcely feel its wonder or its laughter
I'm once again back home in Innisfree.
I wander o'er green hills through dreamy valleys
And find a peace no other land could know
I hear the birds make music fit for angels
And watch the rivers laugh as they flow.

But dreams don't last, though dreams are not forgotten
And soon I'm back to stern reality
But though they pave the footpaths here with gold-dust
I still would choose my isle of Innisfree.

AMHRAN NA BHFIANN

Cois bánta réidhe, ar árdaibh sléibhe,
Ba bhuachach ár sinsir romhainn,
Ag lámhach go tréan fé'n sár-bhrat séin
Tá thuas sa ghaoith go seolta.
Ba dhúchas riamh d'ár gcine cháidh
Gan iompáil siar ó imirt áir,
'S ag siúl mar iad i gcoinne námhad
Seo libh, canaídh Amhrán na bhFiann.

Curfá:–

A bhuíon nách fann d'fhuil Ghaeil is Gall,
Sin breacadh lae na saoirse,
Tá scéimhle 's scanradh i gcroíthe namhad,
Roimh ranna laochra ár dtire.
Ár dtinte is tréith gan spréach anois,
Sin luisne ghlé san spéir anoir,
'S an bíobha i raon na bpiléar agaibh:
Seo libh, canaídh Amhrán na bhFiann.

Curfá:–

Published by WALTONS

THE SOLDIER'S SONG (Amhran Na Bhfiann)

We'll sing a song, a soldier's song; With cheering, rousing chorus,
As round our blazing fires we throng; The starry heavens o'er us,
Impatient for the coming fight; And as we wait the morning's light,
Here in the silence of the night; We'll chant a soldier's song.

Chorus:–

Soldiers are we; Whose lives are pledged to Ireland,
Some have come; From a land beyond the wave,
Sworn to be free; No more our ancient sire-land
Shall shelter the despot or the slave
Tonight we man the 'bhearna bhaoil"; In Erin's cause, come woe or weal,
'Mid cannons' roar and rifles peal; We'll chant a soldier's song.

In valley green, on towering crag; Our fathers fought before us,
And conquered 'neath the same old flag; That's proudly floating o'er us.
We're children of a fighting race; That never yet has known disgrace,
And as we march, the foe to face; We'll chant a soldier's song.

Chorus:–

Sons of the Gael! Men of the Pale!; The long watched day is breaking,
The serried ranks of Inisfail; Shall set the Tyrant quaking.
Our camp fires now are burning low; See in the east a silv'ry glow,
Out yonder waits the Saxon foe; So chant a soldier's song.

Chorus:–

Published by WALTONS

MARY FROM DUNGLOE

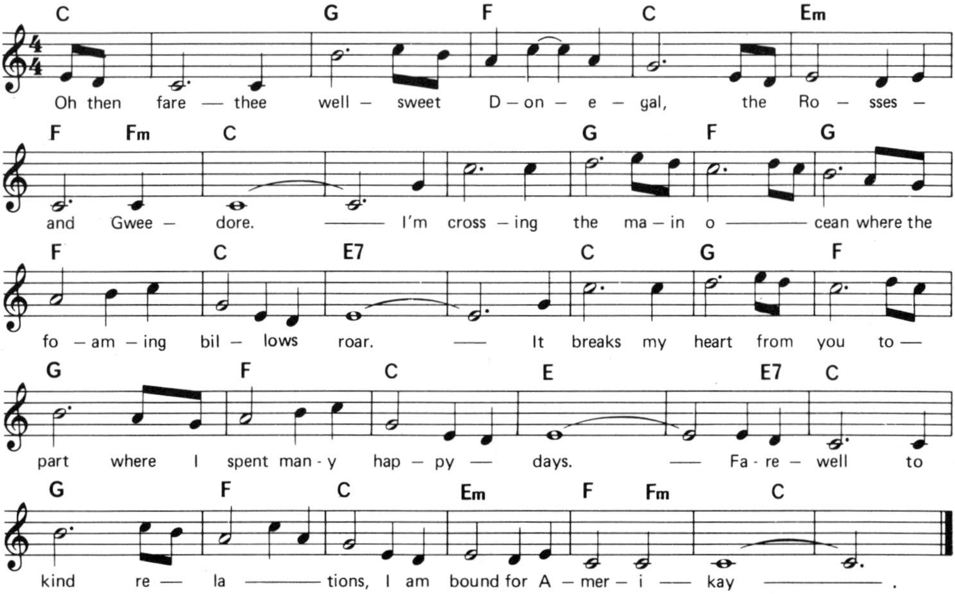

Oh then Mary you're my heart's delight, my pride and only care
It was your cruel father, would not let me stay here
But absence makes the heart grow fond, and when I am over the main
May the Lord protect my darling girl, 'till I return again.

And I wish I was in sweet Dungloe, and seated on the grass
And by my side a bottle of wine, and on my knee a lass
I'd call for liquor of the best, And I'd pay before I'd go
And I'd roll my Mary in my arms, in the town of sweet Dungloe.

Published by THREE CANDLES MUSIC